Wicca

Magic

MW01579003

Ultimate Wiccan book to perform rituals with Herbs, Flowers and Essential Oils. Recipes for Self-Power, Love, Success, and Luck.

All You Need to Know to Create your Wiccan Garden.

EMILY STONE

Contents

© Copyright 2019 by Emily Stone - All rights reserved.

This content is provided with the sole purpose of providing relevant information on a specific topic for which every reasonable effort has been made to ensure that it is both accurate and reasonable. Nevertheless, by purchasing this content you consent to the fact that the author, as well as the publisher, are in no way experts on the topics contained herein, regardless of any claims as such that may be made within. As such, any suggestions or recommendations that are made within are done so purely for entertainment value. It is recommended that you always consult a professional prior to undertaking any of the advice or techniques discussed within.

This is a legally binding declaration that is considered both valid and fair by both the Committee of Publishers Association and the American Bar Association and should be considered as legally binding within the United States.

The reproduction, transmission, and duplication of any of the content found herein, including any specific or extended information will be done as an illegal act regardless of the end form the information ultimately takes. This includes copied versions of the work both physical, digital and audio unless express consent of the Publisher is provided beforehand. Any additional rights reserved.

Furthermore, the information that can be found within the pages described forthwith shall be considered both accurate and truthful when it comes to the recounting of facts. As such, any use, correct or incorrect, of the provided information will render the Publisher free of responsibility as to the actions taken outside of their direct purview. Regardless, there are zero scenarios where the original author or the Publisher can be deemed liable in any fashion for any damages or hardships that may result from any of the information discussed herein.

Additionally, the information in the following pages is intended only for informational purposes and should thus be thought of as universal. As befitting its nature, it is presented without assurance regarding its prolonged validity or interim quality. Trademarks that are mentioned are done without written consent and can in no way be considered an endorsement from the trademark holder.

Introduction

Congratulations on purchasing Wicca Herbal Magic: Ultimate Wiccan book to perform rituals with Herbs, Flowers and Essential Oils. Recipes for Self-Power, Love, Success, and Luck. All you need to know to create your Wiccan Garden. And thank you for doing so.

Set out to explore the magic of herbs with Wicca, a set of beliefs, rituals, and traditions that has swept across the Western world since the mid-twentieth century. Immerse yourself in a system of belief that will connect you back to nature and to the spiritual realm, all while undertaking self-care and personal empowerment. We are all interconnected - with each other, with the earth and the physical realm, with the spiritual energy that flows throughout the universe, and working with herbs and plants is one of the most ancient and natural ways that can serve as a conduit to this understanding. Take advantage of such knowledge to build a life of intention and fulfillment.

One of the most significant parts of Wiccan practice is the use of herbs and plants, the stuff of nature: these materials help you master the art of healing and of becoming one with the harmony of the universe. Once you begin your Wiccan practice, you will start to feel how the spirits and the physical world assist you in producing positive energies and results throughout your life.

With this book, you will learn not only the deeply potent properties of herbs and plants but also how to utilize them - from gardening to preparing teas, oils, baths, and incense - to manifest practical and magical results.

Wicca is, at its very core, an inclusive belief system that emphasizes your relationships with the natural and spiritual realms. Herbal magic is one of the most powerful tools that a Wiccan has at their disposal. Anyone who wishes to channel that energy into a positive and powerful life of intention and achievement can begin by practicing Wicca today!

Chapter 1

Herbal Magic: The Art of Rituals with Herbs

It is fair to suggest that herbs and plants are the oldest tools in the Wiccan magical toolbox: these plant forms evolved millions of years before humans, even, and their healing properties, magical attributes, and deadly potential have long been known to practitioners of all forms of medicine, magic, and shamanism. Evidence of herbal rituals and medical applications has been found in nearly every pre-historic and ancient civilization that has been discovered. Contemporary rituals surrounding herbs can also be found almost everywhere, from the soothing effects of chamomile tea purchased all over the Western world, to the bracing mint tea consumed throughout the Middle East, to the tea ceremonies practiced throughout Asia. In addition, the practice of smudging—burning particular herbs, like sage and rosemary, to purify a space—is employed in various belief systems. Herbs have also been touted as miracle cures, aiding in everything from better sleep to smoother joints to migraine treatments, with the tacit approval of modern Western-style medicine. Finally, we find herbs growing everywhere in community and personal gardens, on windowsills and in pots; we use herbs in cooking with regular abandon, as they both provide a sense of healthy wellness to our meals and a refreshing lift. They have moved beyond garnish into main event, even in the most staid of kitchens.

Of course, practitioners of alternative medicines and variant religions have known about and utilized herbs in a multitude of ways throughout the centuries. The fact that they are a mainstream component of every urbanite's kitchen throughout the globe only makes them that much easier to incorporate into alternate healing rituals or magical ceremonies: not everyone owns a cauldron or a crystal, but nearly everyone has a handful of herbs at their hand, and this gives them a credence that other Wiccan branches of magic don't immediately have.

Within Wiccan practice, the understanding of what constitutes an "herb" is more expansive than what the scientist or botanist would sanction. While herbs, scientifically speaking, are relegated to "any seed-bearing plant which does not have a woody stem and dies down to the ground after flowering." Within the pagan, Wiccan, and alternative medicine communities, however, the term "herb" constitutes any plant material that is practical and useful, from medicinal qualities to cooking potions to casting spells to creating aromas to wearing and using in particular rituals. Thus, when we use the term "herb," for the purposes of this book, this could include other plants that are technically not herbs (flowers, pine needles, mystical plants), as well as spices and other materials from nature that are dried or otherwise preserved for ritual use (cinnamon, cloves, citrus peels, and so on). An herbal remedy or potion or sachet often contains natural elements that are not, again strictly speaking, herbs—still, they are integrated into what we consider herbal magic in general.

Part of the reason that plants, herbs, and other natural ingredients like spices are so integral to Wiccan practice is that these organic compounds embody and symbolize the four classical elements—earth, air, water, and fire—that are central to Wiccan teaching. They must start their life cycle as seeds, nurtured by the earth element and her attendant minerals; they need water to grow and sustain that life; they need the "fire" of sunlight in order to photosynthesize and survive; and they need the elements in the air to convert carbon dioxide into oxygen—the very process that keeps animal life alive. Essentially, plant life represents the life cycle, the seasonal journey, the Wheel of the Year in miniature; the death of one plant nurtures the soil and the life of another, as the endless cycle of birth, death, and rebirth continues throughout time. This is in harmony with humans and animals who help to spread their seeds and propagate their species. Truly, this is at the heart of all Wiccan practice; the only element missing in this explanation is the realm of the spirits— and who could truly argue that the spark of life isn't clearly the spark of the divine? Indeed, nearly *all* Wiccan magic could, at base, be considered some form of herbal magic.

Finally, the power of herbal magic is enhanced and clarified by our growing understanding of how plants actually live and breed—and, yes, communicate. Age-old assumptions that plants were non-conscious entities, unaware of their environment, and unable to communicate have been shattered by contemporary work with plants that reveal, instead, that plants have an intelligence all their own. Of course, many could easily argue that this is what pagans and shamans and witches have known throughout the ages—indeed, that is fundamental to much of their healing and spiritual practices—but this knowledge has been buried by scientific misconceptions going back to the eighteenth century and the advent of materialism. More contemporary scientific discoveries have found that plants of all kinds communicate with each other via all kinds of sophisticated means, not least being an underground "internet" of roots and signals that allow plants to share nutrients, distribute water, warn of danger, and heal one another across distances (some scientists with a gift for puns came up with "wood-wide web" to describe this fascinating phenomenon). Plants are truly miraculous entities, and with the right training and knowledge, they can be put to various magical uses by anyone wishing to follow the Wiccan way.

Magic and Medicine

Wiccan magic is predicated on the notion that we are all interconnected—humans, nature, spirits—in ways that produce particular kinds of energies with which we can direct our intentions. That is, there would be no Wicca without the fundamental belief in the Mother Goddess (or Mother Earth, or simply, Earth) and the Horned God (or Sun God, or simply, Solar Power). You do not necessarily have to personify these deities to understand that their energies create the divine spark of life, and that we are but one mere part of this cosmic dance. Plants, in their sheer diversity and ubiquitous presence within human experience, are one of the constant natural elements with which Wiccan beliefs, rituals, and magic work.

Creating your own Wiccan garden (see Chapter 4 for more details on this) is one of the best ways that you can connect to your Wiccan powers: you are literally channelling the power of nature, the energies of the universe, by putting your hands in the earth and cultivating seeds that grow into living plants. This communion is, indeed, an ancient and sacred one: without the harvest, simply put, humanity ceases to exist. Without the harvest, humankind never evolves beyond the primitive hunter-gatherer and civilization does not exist. We are intimately tied to plants and the life-giving food they provide whether we practice Wicca or not. Think of this in historical perspective: human society was founded by the fundamental need for food and shelter. Hunter-gatherer societies had only the most tenuous of security, and lives were short and brutal. When the discovery of how to grow grain—one of the few food sources that can be stored for long periods of time—came to humankind, there was a much greater sense of security and community, no longer dominated by the vagaries of nomadic life. With that security came the diversification of society, wherein not everyone had to work to hunt or to gather, or even to work the fields. Populations grew larger with more secure food sources, and the labour force diversified: instead of all citizens working just for the procurement of food, some could become artisans and shamans. This is not to say that shamans didn't exist in hunter-gatherer societies; it is to suggest that the role of "medicine man or woman" becomes a fundamental and crucial feature of developing civilizations. And this feature is intimately linked to the harvest, to the plants and herbs from which we derive our healing abilities and our spiritual rituals.

While the earliest archaeological discoveries of the use of herbs dates back to Neanderthal times, the most significant discoveries trace the use of herbal medicines back to the first civilizations, between 5000 and 10000 years ago. By watching animals and keeping track of the seasonal cycles, the earliest civilizations learned, by trial and error, what herbs worked for what ailments and conditions. Because herbs turned out to be powerful aids to healing, they also came to regarded as sacred material—offerings to the gods often involved a variety of herbs, as gratitude for their properties and plenty. Civilizations in the so-called "Cradle of Civilization" (what we might call Mesopotamia and/or the Middle

East) kept well-documented records of the use of various herbs in medical and ritual application—it is no accident that the Three Kings came bearing frankincense and myrrh for the infant Jesus; these were powerful and well-regarded gifts. There are mentions of the use of herbs within the text of the Old Testament, as well as much cataloguing of the planting and harvesting of the grains so crucial to humankind's very survival.

You can trace the use of herbs back to pre-Biblical times in ancient Egypt, wherein they were used to heal, to make offerings to the gods of the Afterlife, and to assist in the passage of the dead (garlic, opium, and a variety of herbs have been found in tombs across Egypt). In the East, herbal medicine is so culturally entrenched that shops specializing in such remedies and rituals exist in every corner of most of Asia. Still yet, this kind of connection between herbs and medicine, with a whiff of magic, is not considered "alternative" in these places. This applies to the use of herbs and plants in food preparation, as well; the Chinese, Japanese, and Koreans still plan meals and cultivate diets that are primarily focused on balancing yin and yang, creating health and well-being. Native Americans employed certain members of the tribe specifically for the cultivation and use of herbs in medicinal and socio-religious rituals, as well. McDonalds is only a (hopefully short-lived) blip on the dietary radar screen.

This is certainly another aspect of herbal magic that is worth mentioning: the idea that what we eat determines how well or mental and physical states are ordered. This notion fell out of favour in the West, to a large extent, due mostly to the rise of industrial agriculture and commercial industries. Created by the military-industrial complex that grew out of World War II, canned and dehydrated foods, highly processed ingredients, and the use of petrochemicals came to dominate the American landscape of eating. Thus, as one might expect, certain kinds of diseases linked to "lifestyle"—heart disease, diabetes, cancer—flourished. We are just now returning to an understanding of the link between our diets—and not merely that, but how our diets are actually produced, transported, and consumed—are fundamental to our health and well-being. To state what might now be the obvious, we are what we eat. Numerous studies over the last couple of decades reveal that this isn't merely a matter of physical health: students who are given healthy lunch food at schools are less disruptive, more productive, and fair better overall, in and out of school. In addition, families who eat dinner together are more likely to stay together and foster success for each member. This is all to say that the link between Wiccan herbal magic and the medicinal powers of food goes beyond a particular niche of our cultural experience; herbal medicine—treating what we eat as sacred property—is as integral to our social success as ever.

Even contemporary medicine still relies on a wide variety of plant material for its potency and efficacy. It should be acknowledged that aspirin is derived from willow bark, an ancient analgesic that has now turned into a billion dollar industry. The synthetic opioids that can be both miraculous healers and deadly addictions were originally created from poppy plants (remember Odysseus and his men getting stuck in the land of the lotus-eaters: poppy plants). Thus, the distancing of modern medicine to the natural world is very recent development and should be viewed both with appreciation (modern advances in medicine have certainly improved life outcomes, for the most part) and with healthy suspicion. The ancient mystique surrounding herbal magic is not mere folklore; it has its roots, pun intended, in a deep understanding of how nature and spirit combine in the physical realm to produce magical results.

In terms of contemporary Wiccan practice, herbal magic is very practical magic, hands-on and straightforward. They are infinitely useful, employed in spellwork, ritual practice of all kinds, magical crafts (such as dream pillows and spell jars), altar conception, and kitchen craft (teas, tinctures, potions, and other foods). Growing your own herbs allows you to direct and channel that energy in light of your own intention from the very beginning. Throughout this book, we will discuss which plants are the most magically conducive plants to grow and how to plant and cultivate them, as well as how to prepare various magical implements with herbs in teas, oils, baths, incense, and in the kitchen generally.

Shamanism and Other Pioneering Work

Shamanism is a form of religious or ritual practice that emphasizes a connection between ourselves and the spiritual realm that surrounds us. It often seeks out altered states of mind that allow us to look beyond the material world into another plane, and this practice is frequently done through the use of herbs and other plants, as well as rhythmic chanting, musical ceremony, and meditation. Contrary to popular belief, shamanism is not associated solely with Native American culture (though it certainly maintains a strong presence therein), and it is found in various forms throughout the world.

Having no particular codified code of beliefs, shamanism is more of a way of thinking about the world in holistic terms—we humans are but a miniscule part within the natural and spiritual realms— and practicing certain rituals and behaviors that align with this way of thinking. Animal totems are often a part of shamanic tradition, in addition to the ubiquitous use of plants and herbs. Shamans have been called by many names—medicine men/women, gurus, spirit guides—but the common denominator is the belief that the divine can be found all around us and that everything we encounter in the world possesses a kind of energy and significance.

Within Wiccan practice, the idea of shamanism influences both its fundamental belief system and its use of herbal magic, meditation, and attention to nature's cycles (phases of moon, seasonal events). The idea of staying grounded and connected to your natural surroundings is also central to both systems. The best shamanic Wiccans are able to tap into the universal energy directly, have an unusual access to the divine, and channel peaceful energy, manifesting a world of intention and well-being. The use of plants and herbs in creating this world is crucial, as explored further in Chapter 2.

In contemporary circles, there are plant pioneers also at work to revive and legitimate the use of herbal magic and other natural materials to bring about a more connected and healthier world. This is a timely movement that takes full advantage of the increasing concern and conversation about climate change and the potential disastrous consequences that come with that. Bringing together a group of diverse people with diverse backgrounds creates a backdrop wherein new and innovative approaches to 21st century problems can be explored. At the core of this is a firm belief in and understanding of the plant's role in our holistic existence. That is, plants are not more important than we are, nor are we more important than plants; we must exist together harmoniously in order to cultivate and manifest good intentions and results.

There are various groups working to raise awareness of the endemic value plants and herbs—and nature in general— throughout the country and the world. Wiccans are only one such group that focus on the power of plants and herbs. This vision of herbal magic extends to include environmental conservation and justice, as well as seeks to help us restore a sense of balance to a world in which we have lost sight of ancient wisdom and the respect necessary to be good stewards of the earth. In reconnecting to this vision in a very personal way—understanding your relationship to nature, seeking balance in your intentions and lifestyle, cultivating a garden, and utilizing herbal magic in your practice—you become a practitioner of the highest order.

Chapter 2

Your Relationship to Nature: Nurturing Your Energy

It is a given, within Wiccan circles, that our relationship with nature is both reciprocal and interactive. It is reciprocal in that what we give to nature, it gives back to us, intertwining our respective fates: without plants, we don't breathe; without plants and/or animals, we don't eat; without us, plants don't breathe; without us, plants don't propagate (at least as successfully). Thus, this mutual entanglement should give rise to respect and a sense of responsibility for the stewardship of the land and all it grants us. It is interactive in the best possible sense: the history of humankind can actually be easily told as a history of cultivation and a continuum of natural forces. Alas, modern day technology has divorced many of us from this relationship—which has the added impact of separating us from the larger spiritual forces in the universe, as well—and it is one of the great feats of Wicca to encourage us to start reconnecting with nature and the universe in this manner.

There are also several principles that form the core of Wiccan belief, followed to some degree or another by any of the Wiccan offshoots to which one might belong. First, rituals are invoked to commune with nature, to harmonize with the natural rhythms of the cosmos. This is often marked by an adherence to the phases of the moon and the changing of the seasons. Second, the desire to live in harmony with nature—particularly given our superior intellect as human beings—is emphasized in all aspects of worship and daily life. Third, there is an acknowledgment that power beyond our basic understanding exists in the world; some may call it "supernatural," though within Wiccan circles, this is simply considered a part of the larger power of nature that has been suppressed or ignored by mainstream modern religion and science. The use of the fundamental four elements—earth, air, water, and fire—is central to Wiccan practice, along with their correspondence to the four cardinal directions—north, south, west, and east—and their association with the feminine divine (earth, water) or the masculine divine (air, fire). When all of these elements work in balance, Wiccan power is at its height.

In sum, Wiccans revere nature and natural processes, holding pantheistic views—that god or spirit resides, at least in part, in nature. Belief in a Mother Goddess runs through all strains of Wiccan thought, sometimes in counterpoint to the Horned God, a male deity that is also connected to nature. Thus, Wiccan belief is also polytheistic—that there is not one ultimate god or spirit that dominates the pantheon (if you even adhere to such language or concept). There are also particular rituals that the vast majority of Wiccan followers participate in, such as solstice festivals and equinox observations, as well as observing the phases of the moon as sacred movements of time and spirit.

The way in which Wiccan magic works is to channel the energy derived from the natural and spiritual realms, in combination with your own energy, power, and intention. Thus, in order to practice Wicca successfully, a basic understanding of how we connect with our own energies is important. Communing with nature is one first, basic step toward practicing Wicca herbal magic, while the second is to learn about our own energy centers and how to utilize them.

Often called "chakras," familiar to many of us from yoga practice or Indian beliefs, these energy centers are both associated with particular parts of our physical existence (heart, brain, other organs) and with our spiritual existence (root, mind, abstract concepts). These chakras work in harmony to increase the flow of energy throughout our bodies and minds, keeping us connected to the spirit inherent in nature and the universe. There are seven main chakras—seven being a sacred number to multiple cultures—that form our understanding of how energy is utilized, maintained, and cycled through the body.

- ❖ **Root chakra**: the physical location of the root chakra is at the base of your spine, keeping you grounded and stable; it also resides near the perineum, giving it associations with birth and origins. It is no coincidence that the word "root" implies family (our roots) and nature in general (roots as life source). The root chakra is the most basic energy centers, and from it everything else important to our lives flows. Therefore, it is vitally important to keep your root chakra healthy, with self-care and grounded meditation; it also thrives on protein for the generation of its energy. When the root chakra is damaged, the manifestations include anxiety and fear, a feeling of disconnection to yourself and the world around you, and deep aching pains in bones or joints.

❖ **Sacral chakra**: in contrast to the grounded stability of the root chakra, the sacral chakra is associated with fluidity and movement. Located at the base of the abdomen, the sacral chakra corresponds to the womb in women; thus, it is key to attraction and reproduction. It is also considered the seat of creative thinking and emotional well-being. To keep your sacral chakra healthy, you must indulge in pleasurable activity (sensual or sexual) and cultivate your creative energy. When you sacral chakra is weak, you often suffer from boredom and a lack of inspiration, as well as impotence and bladder or kidney issues.

❖ **Solar plexus chakra**: your solar plexus is located in the upper abdomen, at the bottom of your rib cage, and it represents vitality and confidence. The solar plexus chakra can ignite our inner fires and passions and help us bolster our self-esteem for transformative events. You can tap your solar plexus chakra for a quick boost of energy any time of the day. The solar plexus chakra is kept healthy by a strong sense of self-worth and trust in one's self; it is fed by starches that keep it strong. If your solar plexus chakra is out of balance, then you feel vulnerable and prone to weakness and can suffer from digestive issues.

❖ **Heart chakra**: physically located at the central point of our body, the heart chakra radiates outward to encompass our arms and hands, mimicking circulation. The heart chakra is associated with compassion and empathy for others, as well as unity in relationships and balance in ourselves. Without love—for self, for others, for nature, and for spirit—our heart chakra suffers. Wiccan magic contains lots of love remedies and spells to help and heal our heart chakra, as it is so crucial to our emotional well-being. The heart chakra particularly thrives on green plants and herbs, so feed it well. When you heart chakra is out of balance, you often feel self-loathing and loneliness, and it can affect the physical health of your heart and lungs.

❖ **Throat chakra**: located, obviously, in the throat region, this chakra symbolizes communication—not just between yourself and others or yourself and nature but also between your mind/soul and body. The throat chakra allows us to listen, as well as speak—listening being a key component of good communication—in addition to promoting self-expression via song and poetic means. The throat chakra is kept healthy through true self-expression and is nurtured physically through the consumption of fruit. If your throat chakra is disordered, then you will have difficulty communicating and taking steps for positive self-care; it can impact your thyroid and make you susceptible to colds, as well.

❖ **Third Eye chakra**: located in the middle of our forehead, the third eye makes its presence in many different cultural belief systems. The seat of thinking and intuition, the third eye chakra is also associated with imagination and spiritual vision, even clairvoyance. We gain insight by engaging this chakra, as it allows us to see beyond our material plane to the spiritual. The third eye chakra is kept healthy by maintaining awareness and connection with ourselves and the natural, spiritual realms. When the third eye is "closed," so to speak, we may find ourselves confused or stymied by poor decision-making skills; it can also create headaches and eyestrain.

❖ **Crown chakra**: located at the top of the head, the crown chakra is the balancing opposite of the root chakra: as the root chakra keeps us grounded to the earth and stable in our being, the crown chakra opens us up to the universe beyond. We use the crown chakra when meditating, and it is associated with wisdom, transcendence, and higher consciousness. This chakra is not nourished by foods but rather by the pursuit of curiosity and the continuous desire to learn. When the crown chakra is out of balance, we find ourselves feeling apathetic and close-minded, unable to accept new ideas or difference.

All of your chakras must work together to keep the flow of energy moving throughout your body and connected to natural forces without. Your entire body contains immense amounts of energy; these regions are the gatekeepers wherein that energy is at its most concentrated. They assist in a continuous exchange of energy that connects the transcendent crown chakra to the emotional heart chakra down to the stable root chakra. When one or more of these chakras is damaged or out of balance, the entire body suffers from the lack of flow. This is why maintaining chakra health is crucial to Wiccan practice—without the ability to conduct your intention through free-flowing energy, then magical intention sits dormant. The connection to your own energy centers is as important to any kind of Wiccan magic as is the connection to the natural world outside.

There are a variety of ways in which you can foster the development of your own energy and a greater understanding of your connection to the natural world. All of these activities will be of use when you begin to start using plants and herbs in your ritual and magical practice. Try some of the following ideas to promote your energy and well-being, involving you more deeply with Wiccan beliefs and practices.

- ❖ As is central to Wiccan belief, there is no one set of principles or ideas that dominate to the exclusion of others. Read widely when determining your ideal Wiccan practice, or seek out podcasts or vlogs to expose yourself to the wide world of Wicca.
- ❖ Seek out Wiccan and pagan festivals near you: they occur regularly throughout the country, usually during Wiccan Sabbats (the eight holidays sacred to the Wiccan calendar), and allow you to connect with a broad community of Wiccan-minded thinkers and practitioners. Communing with others can be as important as communing with nature for the development of your power.
- ❖ If you don't happen to be located near a festival or have the resources to attend, then you might consider reaching out to your local community via social media or other local resources. There are Wiccans living and practicing in communities all over the country, even small towns and rural areas. When connecting with these people, be careful to use your best judgment and be respectful of others' spaces and commitments.
- ❖ If you have the resources, visit Wiccan sacred sites or pagan-style centers. These are also located throughout the country and will be able to connect you with a larger

community, as well as provide educational materials and, in some cases, classes and/or meetings to assist you in developing your Wiccan practice.

❖ If such a place doesn't serve your immediate area, search the internet for practical resources that offer classes, seminars, or other learning experiences to gain insight into regular Wiccan practice and ritual. Investigate these sources thoroughly before enrolling; be sure that they are both legitimate and conducive to what you are specifically looking for.

❖ Finally, simply spend some quality time, Wicca-style: commune with nature by taking a walk or visiting a park; meditate (outdoors, if feasible) to connect with your own energies while learning how to channel those without; start cultivating your herb garden (the following three chapters will get you started) and learning to use the magic of plants to manifest your own intentions.

Chapter 3

The Power of Plants: Utilizing the Best

While all plants and herbs are considered sacred to some degree within Wiccan beliefs, there are some that are endowed with more powerful energies and, thus, more practical usage than others. Each plant contains its own particular properties, conducive to particular kinds of spells, rituals, and intentions. Besides healing, plants and herbs are used in love spells, Sabbat rituals, protective charms, and for self-empowerment. As stated before, Wiccans are not the only group utilizing plants for healing and other purposes; indeed, many of us suck on eucalyptus cough drops to soothe a sore throat or drink a cup of tea or coffee to help tamp down a headache.

Herbs and plants also have a specific vibration about them, an energy signature, and when blended in particular ways, can bring about a balance of humours and energies to cure many ills, whether they be physical, emotional, or spiritual. Later in the book, we will look at some of the various recipes that can be concocted to use herbs for just about any Wiccan ritual or practice you can conjure. Below are some of the most powerful herbs used frequently in Wiccan circles.

Basil

Basil is an oft-used herb, a potent potential medicine and an all-purpose protective shield. It is most frequently used in spells or applications for protection, and can be used along with or in place of sage for smudging (ridding a space of negative energy). It is also, partly because of its bright green color and strong aroma, associated with courage and fertility; carrying it in your wallet attracts wealth, according to some. It is also used in healing rituals, along with other plants and spices. Basil can be brewed into a tea or made into a tincture; like mint, it eases the stomach and aids in digestion. It is used to make essential oils and incense, as well. Dried basil shows up in any number of spells and rituals.

Thyme

Another powerful herb, thyme is used in a number of applications. Not only does it get rid of negative energy—it helps to eliminate waste in the physical body, as well—but it also encourages sleep and fosters psychic energy. It is frequently employed in purification rituals and cleansing baths, while occasionally being used in healing spells. Its material chemistry reveals it to have powerful antiseptic properties, as well as serving as a diuretic (hence the connection with expelling negative energy). It has been used in folk remedies for thousands of years, to treat everything from inflammation to sore throats and infections. Thyme, like many herbs, can aid in digestion and has been used to treat digestive illnesses and parasites through the ages. If you stuff it in a pillow, it is said to relieve nightmares, and it makes for an effective insect repellant to boot.

Cinnamon

Technically a spice, cinnamon is in the herbal magic family of Wiccan practitioners for its ability to ward off bad energies and augment spiritual power. A bold herb, it can be used in prosperity spells and can increase sexual drive for some. It has been used as a digestive aid throughout the centuries—hence why cinnamon is regularly used in desserts and other after dinner treats in cultures spanning the globe. Generally speaking, cinnamon possesses healing qualities, and its strong scent and potent attributes make an excellent accompaniment, especially in oil tinctures, to any ritual or spell. Cinnamon was sometimes strung from doorways to promote the flow of energy and to keep out bad spirits. Its association with the winter holidays is no accident: not only does it aid digestion after the heavy celebratory meals, but it also promotes strong spiritual connections through the long, dark days and into the new year.

Sage

The most common application of sage in contemporary practice is in the use of smudging, getting rid of negative energy in a particular space. It has powerful protective properties, as well as associations with fertility and longevity. Because of its reputation as a protective herb, it is frequently used in healing and general well-being spells. Infused into honey or wine, sage is thought to ease colds and soothe digestion. It also contains attributes that make it good for skin rashes or infections; use it in a cream or a compress to apply directly to the skin.

Rosemary

Rosemary is thought to improve memory in addition to its purported healing and protective abilities. It can be used to enhance intellectual capacities and promote good sleep (one thinks these go hand-in-hand). Because of its antiseptic properties, it is excellent in minor healing applications, and it also works as a mild stimulant, giving a boost of energy when ingested. If you burn rosemary and jasmine together, then you create an atmosphere conducive to recuperation from all kinds of hard work and illness. You can also use rosemary for a quick purification before you begin a ritual or spell: if you don't have the time to do a full ritual bath or cleansing, just rub some dried rosemary between your palms before you begin.

Nutmeg

Magically speaking, nutmeg is alleged to increase clairvoyance and provide psychic visions; indeed, taken in large quantities, nutmeg can be a mild hallucinogen (however, this is not recommended, as the quantity needed to induce any hallucinatory affects is potentially harmful to the throat, lungs, and body. Also, it's overwhelmingly strong). Scientifically speaking, nutmeg has numerous proven benefits: it can act as an antioxidant, repairing the body's energy from the inside out, as well as an antibacterial; it reduces inflammation, just as other warm spices like cinnamon do; it is potentially effective in increasing sexual drive; and some results show that it helps regulate blood sugar and increases circulation, aiding in cardiovascular health.

Mugwort

One of the most traditional of plants used in shamanic practice throughout history, mugwort is a member of the Artemisia species, which flourishes in many forms across the globe. It is thought to improve psychic abilities in general and increase clairvoyance in particular. Both the leaves and roots are utilized in making potions and brews to help aid in digestion and the expelling of waste, as well as to provide relaxation. It can be used as a mild sedative and was often employed to stimulate menstruation (in some cases, mugwort was used to get rid of unwanted pregnancy). Some accounts suggest that, if you place mugwort leaves in your shoes during a long journey, you will not get overly fatigued.

Lavender

Lavender is most commonly associated with serenity and calm, making it an ideal herb for promoting meditative states and good sleep. It also assists in fostering clarity of thought and can engender wishes, particularly useful in love potions. Infusions of lavender, as in a tea, act as a mild sedative and can soothe a headache. When made into an oil tincture, lavender can be applied as a mild disinfectant to treat cuts, burns, and scrapes. Because it has such a pleasant aroma, lavender is often added to baths, used as incense, or incorporated into scented candles. It can stimulate the immune system while detoxifying the body, making it an excellent choice for ritual cleansing.

Hibiscus

Not only is this a beautiful flowering plant with a wonderful aroma, hibiscus is also used to make delicious foods and drinks in the kitchen. Common to Mexican cooking—dating from pre-Columbian times—hibiscus has been used to treat fevers and coughs, respiratory and digestive issues. It is used in all manner of feminine treatments, from soothing menstrual cramps to preventing PMS symptoms to assist in a less painful birth. Its brilliant red color connects it both to strength and to blood; thus, it embodies both masculine and feminine properties in balance. Some evidence suggests that it helps in regulating blood pressure.

Elecampane

This plant has a reputation for attracting love; carry a bit of dried elecampane with you and love will seek you out. It is also good for increasing psychic powers when burned and is used in many medicinal brews, both root and leaves. The boiled root can also be used as a tonic to help cure weakness, and the plant itself contains a natural form of insulin so it can be effective in combating diabetic symptoms (though it is no substitute for medical advice and prescription medications). It has been used in shamanic ceremonies as offerings for nature spirits, appeasing the mischievous sprites. Burning it in incense form is also said to enhance meditative states.

Chamomile

Another herb that is frequently used to aid in meditation and to promote serenity in general, chamomile tea is found in grocery stores the world over. Chamomile, in Wiccan circles, is also used as a protective herb when sprinkled across the threshold of your home. This herb is also an anti-inflammatory for minor cuts, scrapes, and burns. It aids in digestion; in tea form, it is mild enough even to give to young children. Tinctures of chamomile can be used as an insect repellant, as well, and planting chamomile in your garden gives your land protection. A person with chamomile in their garden is said to be a guardian of the land.

Bay Laurel

Separate from bay leaves, bay laurel is toxic when ingested; only use it externally as a poultice for healing chest ailments, such as colds or bronchitis. Magically speaking, bay laurel is said to provide wisdom (burn as an incense for this application) and can be used in protective spells. Bay laurel is also an appropriate choice for use in smudging, as it can banish negative energies, as well.

Bay leaves—the kind that you usually have dried in your kitchen—are useful for a wide variety of kitchen applications, and the fresh version of the leaf is both incredibly tasty and potent. These leaves are said to increase dream activity, providing psychic visions.

Dandelion

This common backyard weed is much more interesting than its humble suburban reputation. Once regularly used in wine and tea, dandelion promotes a healthy digestive system, helping to purge bad humors. As long as you are certain that chemicals haven't been applied to the lawns in your area (that includes fertilizers, pesticides, fungicides, any weed killers), you can steep the tops of dandelions in simmering water for about ten minutes to make a tonic for digestion (sweeten with honey, both for taste and for added benefit). Dandelion is considered a welcoming plant, so it opens the flow of energy between you and the spirit world, bringing messages. Thus, it is often used in divination practice.

Other Important Plants

The above are a mere handful of the numerous plants and herbs that have been used in shamanic and pagan traditions of various kinds throughout human history. Nearly all of the common garden herbs we see—basil, sage, rosemary, thyme (as mentioned above), parsley, cilantro, chives, mint—can be used for a multiplicity of ritual practice, spellwork, and healing applications. Garlic is another magical plant that has been usurped into the fantasies of vampire literature as a force to ward off evil, and indeed, that is one of its properties within traditional pagan practice. But, garlic is also an antiseptic and a protective plant, with a potent presence that can be used alongside many herbs.

Depending on what kind of Wicca you practice, certain plants have meaning: for example, grains of all kinds are significant in that they symbolize the life-giving powers of the earth (feminine element) harmonizing with the energy of the sun (masculine element). As discussed previously, grain was the original plant that allowed humankind to settle into civilizations rather than remain in nomadic societies. The grain—wheat, barley, rye, millet, farro, among many others—was revered as a gift from the gods and from the land, and the harvest celebrated as the life-giving event that it most certainly was.

There are other strains of belief that give credence to a variety of sacred herbs and plants. Some shamanic systems call the nine sacred herbs—mugwort, plantain, watercress, bugloss, chamomile, nettle, sweet cicely, fennel, and crab apple—the pathway to the spirits. In some Native American traditions, the trio of corn, tomatoes, and beans are considered sacred; indeed, the Mayan people referred to themselves as "people of the corn," with their fundamental creation myth implying that the gods breathed life into corn turning them into human beings. In Asia, the wide range of sacred and medicinal herbs is literally mind-boggling, numbering in the tens of thousands, and rice is the sacred grain of choice.

The geography from which your ancestors and/or your belief systems come from determines what plants, herbs, and other natural materials you will utilize in your rituals. The benefit to the Wiccan tradition, with its egalitarian syncretism, is that it respects and borrows from all.

Chapter 4
Wiccan Exercise: Creating a Wiccan Garden

As one of the central tenants of Wiccan practice, communing with nature and honoring the fundamental elements should be a part of every Wiccan's daily life. One of the best ways to do this, short of building an outdoor altar or participating in Dionysian style rituals (though both are also quite appropriate), is to set up an outdoor space that incorporates the overarching philosophies of Wicca with the powerful natural magic of plants and herbs. The following ideas give you a sense of how to set up that space, incorporating and arranging crystals, stones, and other Wiccan tools within a natural setting to promote positive energy throughout your outdoor living space. For more ideas on how to bring this energy into your home, read the following chapter on cultivating house plants.

Wiccan Gardening: Harnessing the Power of Herbs

❖ Perhaps the first priority is to consider the perennial magic of nature, of the garden or outdoor space that you can cultivate. Spend some time thinking about the possibilities and the pleasures of utilizing a harmonious garden space: nature itself is magic, and by building a conscious space in which to practice Wicca and understand the connections between all living (and, in the case of stones, inorganic but energetically charged) materials, one can practice some of the highest magic. In addition to utilizing the energy inherent to crystals and stones, a garden can provide herbs that are frequently used in Wiccan spells and rituals; it can harness the renewable energy of the earth and of plants in myriad ways; it can bring about an even greater sense of interconnectedness by arranging organic and inorganic materials in particular ways to promote particular energies and intentions. Think of the garden as your spiritual workshop.

❖ A garden is both a planned and a spontaneous space: on the one hand, you are carving out a particular area—just as you do for your altar indoors—for specific reasons; on the other hand, you are also acknowledging the inadvertent randomness of nature and the inherent power within that entropic energy. Set aside and cleanse a space, of course— smudging is particularly effective in building a garden area—but don't forget to revel in the wildness of how nature responds. Try as you might, weeds will grow in between your carefully placed stones. Keep it tidy as you like or can, but also welcome the natural profusion of life.

❖ While this is not an utter necessity, gardening organically is probably more in keeping with the Wiccan spirit than not. For the home gardener, this all becomes pretty simple: in order to garden organically, you simply need to avoid synthetic fertilizers in favor of natural ones, such as compost, and synthetic pesticides. The home gardener need not worry about sewer sludge, one assumes, though locating your garden away from neighborhood ponds or parks is always a good idea, as areas that are kept up by communities or government-run entities often use synthetic materials; avoiding runoff ensures that your garden maximizes its healthy, organic potential.

* With organic gardening, not only are you utilizing solely natural materials, you are also contributing to positive energies in many well-documented ways: first, using heirloom seeds preserves centuries-old traditions and plant stocks that are disappearing in our hybridized world; second, you are minimizing your carbon footprint, in general, when you use home compost instead of petrochemicals; third, you avoid participating in the creation of monocultures which are vulnerable to pests and diseases (and extinction); fourth, you are resisting the technocratic imposition of genetically modified seeds and organisms in our food supply; fifth, you are supporting farmers and growers (by buying their seeds and materials) that do not utilize questionable labor practices as much of industrial farming does.

* When creating an outdoor space for a Wiccan lifestyle, don't just toss aside the stones and other elements you uncover while clearing your particular space: utilize the

found objects in the creation of your garden's grid and perimeters. These items will hum with local energy and resonate within your space in ways that purchased items cannot. Depending on what you find, you can encircle your sacred space with found stones, be they large or plentiful enough; place them at the corners of your property representing the four cardinal directions for protection and the encouragement of energy flow; plant them purposefully in the ground before an image of the deity to whom you honor. Found stones and other natural materials have a natural attachment to that place; use that energy to conduct positive vibrations and concentrate magical possibilities.

❖ Besides cleansing the space, through a combination of purification rituals and smudging, also consider the power of intentions in words themselves. Begin by sprinkling water—spring not tap—mixed with some lemon (juice or extract) across the garden space to dispel negative energy. Then, sprinkle spring water mixed with some essence of rose to attract positive energies. Smudge with natural herbs (sage is omnipresent for this kind of energy), then consider what you intend the space to be, what intentions you wish it to manifest. Say a quick incantation to bless and inure the space with meaning and intention (you can write this yourself or do a quick internet search for some ideas). Carve words of intention of affirmation into the stones you will arrange within the garden, or till them into the ground. This is about combining the energy of your will and intention with the natural energy that resides and is channeled through your garden space.

❖ You can also convey your intentions—and your potential healing power—to this ground that you have cleared for your sacred practice by the laying of your hands onto the earth. Simply place your palms flat on the earthen surface or on a stone's face and repeat your intention; your hands should grow warm from the flow of energy that you create in conjunction with natural spirits.

❖ This kind of blessing and sacrament can also be achieved through dance and incantatory prayer. When done under the light of the moon, this kind of energy exchange can be especially powerful.

❖ Remember that the soil is food for your plants, and treat it with the care and attention it deserves; after laying down your topsoil, the best way to create a healthy, energetically charged garden is through natural compost. Basically, composting is the method by which you break down organic matter—grass, leaves, food waste—into a kind of fertilizer. The goal is to achieve a balance of particular elements that encourage plant growth and, in some cases, discourage pests and disease. Essentially, compositing takes time, some management, and a conscientious view of reusing materials.

- Aside from your stone configuration, plant herbs and other greenery that have magical uses, such as Artemisia silverfirs or certain varieties of tree. There are numerous flowers that are considered to have magical properties, the rose being only one of them. Don't forget about moon gardens, as well: there are a variety of plants and flowers that bloom under moonlight; these plants are considered especially powerful, in conjunction with the Mother Goddess, and highly auspicious. The uses of magical herbs are boundless within Wiccan practice, and many of them are easily cultivated at home (indoors as well as out), as well as being all the more powerful within your space because you yourself planted your intentions along with the seeds or seedlings. Seeds themselves are highly symbolic of the ritualistic cycle of renewal and rebirth; as such, they can be used as magical objects in and of themselves.

- Doing all of the above has the additional benefit of attracting the birds and the bees. Aside from the obvious association with fertility, both birds and bees are aligned with a long tradition of magical folklore and various kinds of good fortune and energy. Creating a space for living creatures is part of the goal of creating the garden itself.

- In addition, think beyond stones to other natural, mostly "found" objects that can have powerful connections to natural and spiritual realms. While stones are naturally connected to the earth element, shells are associated with water and sticks invoke the element of fire, while feathers signify air. Combining all four elements within your garden creates a significant force of energy.

❖ Among the easiest and arguably some of the most useful plants to cultivate in your garden, herbs are indispensable to Wiccan practice. Additionally, herbs can be readily grown in pots, leaving the bulk of your raised bed to other plants (if using a drip irrigation system, pots are fairly easy to integrate with spot watering emitters). It is undeniably satisfying to simply pop outside and scissor off a small handful of herbs to enhance any meal or use for any ritual during the growing season. And many herbs will return each year—depending on your location—and be some of the first pleasures to be harvested at the start of the next spring.

❖ For those herbs that won't return, either because they are annuals or because your location gets too cold, be sure to pull the plants from your garden at the end of growing season to dry them or make infusions with them (more details on that in Chapter 10): herbs that you grow and dry or infuse into oils yourself are infinitely more powerful to use in your personal rituals and spell work than those that you dry.

❖ Herbs can be either direct seeded or grown from seed and transplanted into your garden, if you like, though herb seeds are typically so tiny that they are difficult to handle. Instead, you can procure seedlings from a reliable local source who uses organic methods. With annual herbs, plant seedlings after the last frost.

❖ Practically speaking, you will need to invest in some tools for successful gardening: a small shed to keep tools and supplies, a couple of pairs of gloves (one pair hearty enough for digging and weeding, one delicate enough for clipping and pruning), a shovel, some rakes (a small hand rake for working between rows and a full-size rake for smoothing soil and making rows), shears and scissors (never pinch off your herbs: this weakens the plant and can introduce disease; clip them instead), and a hand spade for planting and close digging.

❖ Also be aware that your garden is—like the Wiccan Wheel of the Year—never without energy and intention. Just because it is winter and most plants are dormant does not mean that your garden isn't an active place humming with energy. In addition, in most regions of the country, gardening doesn't have to be a spring and summer proposition only; certainly, those times of year are the most productive and abundant, but fall and winter provide their own opportunities. For example, planting certain herbal varieties and foods such as hearty greens (collards, kale, some kinds of spinach) and squashes (butternut, acorn, pumpkin) in late summer will yield a harvest for fall. Apple trees—if you have the room and the patience—are another wonderful fall crop with much magical potency. Late fall is the time to plant certain crops for overwintering, among them garlic and onions, both powerful healing plants with protective powers. Other root vegetables, such as carrots, potatoes, and turnips can be overwintered in many regions. Remember that your pagan ancestors had to depend on being able to harvest—or store—food throughout the year, not just in the abundant months of summer. Respect their traditions by caring for your spiritual garden year-round.

❖ Finally, learn how to ask permission. Be sure to convey your intentions to the found objects and see if/how they respond; this takes time and practice, but it is an important part of learning to be a responsible and powerful Wiccan. Understanding that the natural world responds just as powerfully as does a sentient being is key to harnessing and honoring that power. Also always give gratitude to the earth or the element from which you are gathering energy and intention: this can be a simple thought intention of gratitude or an offering of water, food, or personal item. This recognition kindles and maintains the spirit of interconnection between our individual selves and the natural, spiritual realm which surrounds and nurtures us.

Wiccan Gardening: Utilizing the Power of Crystals and Stones

❖ Using stones and crystals in your garden is an undeniably appropriate and powerful way to direct earthly energies: since these objects come from the earth, it is only natural that they would respond and communicate with it, serving as a conveyance between your intention and the natural realm. Crystals and stones can also impact the health and abundance of the organic materials you grow; using them to promote growth and prevent disease is one of the ways in which your garden can thrive.

❖ Green and brown stones, representative of the earth element and thus intimately connected to the idea of gardening and harvesting, are among some of the most appropriate stones you can use for your garden. These stones not only represent growth and renewal, but also wealth and stability. Emerald, jade, bloodstone, green fluorite, and green calcite are some fertile choices, while smoky quartz, pyrite, tiger's eye, and petrified wood are excellent choices to ground your garden. Yellow stones are associated with the sun, of course, and bring success and confidence to your project: try citrine, amber, and gold topaz, for examples. Blue or grey stones represent the water element, as well as the associations with the mystical powers of the moon: bring a healing, serene element to your garden with moonstone, turquoise, azurite, and lapis lazuli.

* ❖ Also consider the appearance of the stones outside of color, such as their condition or state and their geometric configurations. For example, taking note of whether a stone is tumbled (that is, polished) or raw impacts their use: tumbled stones are frequently used in all kinds of Wiccan practice, of course, from meditation to healing to protection and beyond; raw stones are potentially more fragile but can also be more powerful, more connected to the earth from whence they came. There are also geometric shapes to consider, whether a stone is a pyramid form (suggesting spiritual reach and amplification) or spherical (suggesting limitless access to energetic flow) or cubed (suggesting mindfulness, willpower, and concentration). These considerations will help you choose and arrange stones that are explicitly working to manifest your intentions.

* ❖ Some particular stones that are frequently used in gardens because of their specific associations are as follows:
  * o Moss Agate is ubiquitous in alternative garden, as its nickname, "the gardener's talisman" would suggest. It promotes healthy growth in all manner of plants.
  * o Tree Agate is used to enhance the sense of security and stability in your garden's field of energy. As

trees are symbolic protectors of the earth, so the Tree Agate is a symbolic protector of your garden and space.

o Green Aventurine absorbs negative energy, bringing harmony to a space and protecting it from the ill effects of pollution.

o Aquamarine is used to harness and enhance the beneficial energies of water, mitigating drought (also especially good if you have a water source in your garden, such as a natural pond or water barrel).

o Green Calcite is known as the "stone of encouragement" and can help relax your plants and surroundings, encouraging a thriving, serene garden space.

o Citrine promotes happiness and vibrates with energy and warmth.

o Rhyolite is used to promote resilience and fortitude and would be especially helpful to any garden that is struggling.

o Obviously, pure quartz is the master stone and is useful in almost any instance, a master healer and conductor of positive energy.

❖ Arrange your crystals and stones in clear patterns within your garden, utilizing any number of ideas. For example, arrange stones in deference to the four cardinal directions, with north, south, west, and east represented by their associated elements of earth, air, water, and fire: look to Chapter 3 for an orientation in the varying energies and alliances of particular stones. Or, arrange stones and crystals into a grid pattern with a strong central stone radiating outward to connect to an encircling arrangement of carefully chosen stones; this can look like any number of Wiccan symbols or can be of your own devising.

❖ You can also use your stones as guardians of the garden, placing them around the perimeter of the space just as you would cast a circle around your sacred space for rituals.

❖ Think beyond the ground itself: hang stones from tree branches for protection, or store in the watering can to bring positive energy to what's growing. Line the pathway between the living space and the garden space with stones and crystals to promote the flow of energy between spaces.

❖ Gardens are always seasonal to varying degrees, of course, but think of your stone garden—or the space within your garden reserved for stone arrangements—as a way to honor the various seasons throughout the year, creating patterns of color and shape that correspond to each season of the year. This could also use the four elements and cardinal directions as guidance, as well. Your homage to the Mother Goddess could be an herbal garden marked by green stones representing fertility and brown stones honoring the earth; thus, it would still be lovely in the dead of winter, merely waiting for the rebirth of spring to become full and lively once again. A central stone grid could actually be a guide to what you plant and how you arrange it, as well. Certainly, a stone garden could also be a kind of altar at which you perform rituals out in nature itself; this would be up to you and how much privacy and space you have, of course. Finally, you could simply make a stone garden wherein nature would take its own course; that is, a stone garden is powerful even without planting organic elements, though a combination of organic and inorganic energies is bound to vibrate with higher energies.

There is undeniably something magical about gardening, in general. When we garden with Wiccan intention, using organic methods, this act is not merely about abstract thinking; it is about getting one's hands dirty, literally, working with the earth and the weather in order to feed the body, the mind, and the soul. It is hard to overestimate the kind of respect one gains for where our food comes from until you've worked a farm or a garden. If your children's only experience of food comes from shrink-wrapped packages or orderly supermarket shelves, then it is unlikely that a strong respect for nature will inherently come out of that. Gardening and farming model the ethics of hard work—reveals the "fruits of our labors," quite literally speaking—and creates strong moral considerations regarding waste and carelessness. It is easy to ignore a shriveling head of lettuce in the fridge if you picked it up for a couple of dollars at a corporate run grocery store; it is nearly impossible to let that go when you planted it, nurtured it, and harvested it yourself.

Chapter 5

Wiccan Exercise: Cultivating House Plants

Using nature in your Wiccan practice doesn't necessarily have to be relegated to the outdoors: house plants are not only lovely adornments for a space but they are also potentially bursting with magical properties, as well. In addition, it's simply a good idea to bring living organisms into your space; their positive energy and multiple magical properties bring a flow of energy and natural good will to your space. Many of the tips and techniques for working with plants from the previous chapter can apply here, of course, and some of the herbs that you might plant in a garden can thrive indoors, as well. If you don't have the space for an outdoor garden, then you can easily set up a small herb garden in your kitchen windowsill or other sunny spot in your house. There are also kits available that include grow lamps and other methods of keeping indoor herbs with little fuss or mess (including hydroponically). Whatever you choose, bringing medicinal and magical plants into your home can assist in your Wiccan rituals and spellwork.

Choosing plants is entirely up to your needs, your aesthetic, and your limitations. Many plants are multi-purpose and work well for a variety of spells and potions, so if you are limited by space (or by children and pets or allergy considerations), you should still be able to find a handful of indoor plants that will suit whatever your needs. In terms of aesthetic considerations, thinking about color, texture, and most importantly, arrangement of plants is inherent to Wiccan systems: various colors vibrate with different energies, as do the plants themselves (red for power, orange for vibrancy, yellow for inspiration, green for good fortune, blue for serenity), so calibrate your choices with that rubric partially in mind. Texture also determines how the plants will direct the flow of energy; spiky plants, such as cacti, move energy upward and into the spirit realm, while the long, loping vines of a spider plant keep energy in a flow throughout the home. These factors also play into the decision as to where to place plants throughout your space: a blue flowering plant might be excellent in the bedroom, providing peace and calm for sleep; herbs are, of course, natural to a kitchen window (though if you don't have a kitchen window, any sunny spot will allow them to thrive); protective ferns might be kept near doorways.

You will be most successful with whatever plants you choose if you follow some basic guidelines for care and safety. Many of the plants discussed below are easily available at local garden centers or chain retail outlets; the advantage from buying these plants from a large retail outlet is that they will come with notations about how best to care for the plant, as in how much sunlight and water it needs, as well as warnings regarding its toxicity to pets and children. Buying from local garden centers has the advantage of one-on-one advice—more in-depth knowledge, usually, of how to nurture indoor plants and what to do with them—as well as supporting local growers, if available in your area. There are also some indoor plants and herbs that can easily be cultivated in a DIY fashion: avocado trees, alfalfa and other sprouts, and many herbs can be started from seed. Below you will find a list of indoor plants, their magical properties, and their basic care instructions.

African Violet

This lovely—and tough—plant blooms with blue and/or purple flowers. It radiates a feminine energy and is said to stimulate spirituality. It is relatively easy to take care of, but shouldn't be left out for pets or small children to handle. In previous times, the plant was used as a protection against the mischievous acts of faeries and thus enjoys a continuing reputation as a protector plant.

Aloe

Most of us know about the healing powers of the aloe Vera plant; the sap from mature leaves is highly effective in treating burns, as well as minor cuts and scrapes. Its protective nature also gives it a reputation for repelling negativity, and it is closely associated with the moon and water—thus, another symbol for fertility. Indeed, when you cut a leaf to extract sap, it heals quickly and grows stronger. Placing the aloe plant in a kitchen or other area where lots of activity happens is said to prevent accidents. Its vibrations are so strong that it has earned the nickname, "plant of immortality," and it pulls in positive energies wherever it is kept.

Bamboo

This quick-growing and hardy plant has become somewhat ubiquitous throughout the country today, thanks to the burgeoning popularity of feng shui and Asian philosophy in general. It acts as a purifier of energy, processing negative energy and transforming it into positive; in fact, in many places throughout Asia (and in Hawaii) bamboo grows in great protective forests, a kind of rain forest in miniature. These plants offer balance and serenity, associated with the element of water, and smaller plants are placed throughout spaces to collect good fortune. You will often see bamboo plants near the register of an Asian place of business (along with the inevitable, maneki neko, or good luck cat).

Basil

One of the most oft-used herbs in Wiccan and other pagan magic, basil is an indispensable part of rituals, spells, and food preparations. It is fast growing and easy to care for, as long as it has plenty of sun and some warmth. It has been integral to Western culture since Greco-Roman times, when a house without a basil plant was seen as weak and divided; the basil provides protection as well as magical powers and sustenance. Basil is employed in numerous spells and charms, as well as in potable concoctions; its only limitations, really, is that its actions are considered steady and slow-growing rather than instantaneous. The use of basil requires a constant and stable hand; this is why it's always a good idea to keep one around. It loves the middle part of the garden in summer, basking in the full sunlight and responding well to light pruning. It can be kept indoors, though it will never get quite as large as outdoors in full sun.

Cacti

One of the easiest of plants to care for, the cactus exists in nearly infinite mutations and can be kept alive for the lifetime of its caretaker, in most instances. When situated at all four cardinal directions—north, south, west, and east—these plants keep a house well-guarded. They are also said to ward off envy and malicious actions. Their spines can be dangerous, of course, but if harvested gently and correctly, can be used in spells or charms of protection. They channel the masculine energies of the sun and of Mars, but contrary to popular belief, they do require a bit of tender care: if you pot them in nutrient-rich soil, then they will thrive with only a bit of water on a weekly basis. If you live in a humid environment, then the amount of water they may need will be minimal. Overwatering will cause them to turn a sickly yellowish color, so watch out for that.

Chrysanthemum

This lovely autumnal plant helps us to communicate with our ancestors, and it channels spiritual energy into wisdom. Their lovely fall colors—yellows, golds, oranges, greens—radiate with positive energy and happiness; they bring a sense of well-being to any home. Put these plants about your house in time for autumnal holidays wherein an influx of family and friends might create tension; these helps promote positive energies and relaxation. They make a great centerpiece for a potentially difficult Thanksgiving gathering. Choose several different colors to place in different areas; in addition to the happiness and vibrancy of the golden hues and the good fortune of the green hues, the plants can also be found in purples, encouraging peacefulness and spiritual connection.

Citrus

While most climates will not support the growth of citrus trees long enough to bear fruit, some varieties thrive in indoor climates where they are well-tended. All citrus fruits have antiseptic, cleansing qualities and are used in many rituals for just that purpose. Additionally, the use of citrus peel, either dried or infused in oil, is common in spell work and other magical applications frequently. Lemons, of course, are prized for their cleansing capacity, and their bright yellow color sparks positivity and inspiration; limes are less frequently used, but their bright green color attracts good fortune, and dried limes can be used to stimulate libido; orange trees cannot be grown indoors, but the smaller orange citrus fruit, the kumquat, does well inside and its vibrancy brings positive vibrations and vital energy to any space. With its sweet, edible peel and intensely sour flesh, kumquats are also a symbol of balance; you must eat the fruit whole to enjoy the balance of the extremes.

Cyclamen

This beautiful pink or purple flowering plant should be placed in the bedroom to promote attraction, passion, and fertility. This plant is used frequently in love or attraction spells, as well as in spells designed to increase happiness and joyfulness. The bedroom is also an ideal place for this plant, even if you have no need to increase passion, as it wards off nightmares, as well.

Eucalyptus

Its cleansing properties are well-known, and its antiseptic scent and flavor are agreeably astringent. It wards of negativity, especially envious feelings, and invigorates a space with its strong scent. It is also believed to attract money; thus, you will often find them in businesses. Put one in your home office for similar results. Eucalyptus is used in purification and protection spells, and it is often used in essential oils.

Fern

Ferns are thought to attract good spirits and help to keep the flow of energy moving throughout a space; their presence among other plants will stimulate growth and productivity all around. Ferns are excellent to place near doorways and windows, warding off bad spirits and bringing in the good.

Jade Plant and Other Succulents

Jade plants are ubiquitous in Asia for their ability to bring good fortune. The same is true of a wide variety of succulents, and these plants are thought to bring balance to the more delicate flowering house plants you might keep around. Succulents, like cacti are easy to take care of, but do be aware that the jade plant doesn't appreciate full sunlight. This is what makes it an ideal subject for a sunny windowsill rather than a garden plant.

Jasmine

This flowering plant is used in spells and aromatherapies throughout the world, not to mention its ubiquitous use as the delicate perfume infused in green tea. It is thought to enhance attractiveness, so it is frequently used in self-care spells. It also functions as a healing plant, helping with emotional disappointments and depression. It serves as a conduit between the physical and the spiritual realms and, as such, is welcome anywhere in the home.

Mint

One of the fastest-growing and aggressively hardy of all herbs, mint is an all-purpose plant to keep around: it functions as a protector, a cleanser, a healer, and a promoter of positive energy. It is infused in a tea, alone or in conjunction with other ingredients, to perform all of the aforementioned magic. It likes full sun, as well, so you can bring it indoors to keep it through winter, if you pay special attention to it. If planted outdoors, mint will return the next spring—but use caution, as mint will quickly take over any space in which it is planted. Best to keep it confined to a pot. Also be aware that there are many varieties of mint (besides spearmint and peppermint, there is also chocolate, lemon, lime, cinnamon, and so on), as well as adjacent members of the mint family that are also useful in numerous magical applications (lemon verbena, for one).

Orchids

These beautiful and delicate flowers are used in love spells, primarily. They are well worth the effort if you want to invest it, but they are notoriously difficult to grow. Consult a local expert for assistance if you'd like to tackle this wonderfully mysterious moon plant.

Sage

Another hardy herb, sage is used frequently in the practice of smudging, wherein you burn a bundle of dried herbs to waft the smoke throughout a space clearing out negative energy. It is easy to grow both indoors and out, and can be used in kitchen applications, as well. Most often, sage is used dried as its texture and aromas can be unpleasant when fresh.

Spider Plant

These fast growing and virtually indestructible plants are symbolic of regeneration and provide protection to the home. You can divide a spider plant, placing a limb in another pot of soil, and it will rapidly regrow into another full plant, no need for roots. Place these in windows to bring in positivity, keep watch, and move the energy through the space.

Thyme and Other Herbs

Thyme is used in lots of healing rituals, particularly potent in issues of the respiratory system. It is also a purifying herb and can be used in rituals that promote self-confidence. Another herb associated with purification and strength is rosemary, which, like thyme and sage, is excellent used in dried form. Oregano is another health-giving herb which is employed in potions and teas. Chives are also a resilient herb which will come back over winter; the flowers can be used to make healing teas, as well.

Chapter 6

Practical Magic: Preparing Teas

Undoubtedly, one of the most common ways in which to use herbs is to steep them in flavorful and powerful teas. These teas are used, for the most part, as healing draughts or magical boosters, and can be quite delicious as well as magical. Most often, herbs are dried before use in teas, but occasionally they can be used fresh; in certain cases, a tea can be one way in which to preserve an abundance of herbs for use at various times. Chapter 10, on The Wiccan Kitchen, will give you more preservation tips and techniques. As with much regarding the use of herbs, the making of herbal teas and tisanes has a long and proven history, and there does not exist a corner of the globe that doesn't still utilize herbs, fruits, flowers, and other plants in making delicious and magical brews: from mate in South America to medicinal teas in China to the ubiquitous mint tea throughout the Middle East to chamomile tea in the Western pantry, the practical magic of preparing teas is sought out the world over. The following advice and recipes utilize Wiccan understandings of the power of particular herbs and other related ingredients. You can also visit Chapter 11 for a Table of Correspondence showing what herbs and plants are related to what properties; this can assist you in creating your own unique teas for your own particular intentions.

For best results, drink one or two cups of the herbal blends a day; any more can potentially cause some negative side effects (many herbs are diuretics, which can affect other medications, as well as electrolyte balances). Don't drink a particular blend of tea for more than a week or so. Some herbs can become toxic when consumed in large amounts, as well; these are noted below. Use extra precaution with tinctures, as these highly concentrated concoctions can interfere with other medications and can easily become toxic if consumed in large amounts.

- ❖ **Teas**: making teas is a very straightforward procedure. Simply steep your ingredients in hot—not boiling—water for a few minutes, then strain and sweeten, if you like. Boiling water will often "cook" the ingredients, rendering them less effective and giving them a bitter or overly vegetal taste; instead, heat your water to boiling, then let it cool for about two minutes before pouring over your ingredients. This gets it to about the right temperature. When steeping, you can put your ingredients in cheese cloth that has been knotted together or in a mesh tea ball, or you can simply strain the ingredients through a fine-mesh strainer once you have finished the steeping process. In many parts of the world, straining isn't followed at all; rather, the ingredients are topped off with another round of really hot water to make a second cup. This is up to you, as the longer the ingredients are left to steep, the stronger the tea becomes, and a second cup will invariably be less potent than the first should you re-steep. This is as much about habit and preference as it is about potency and usefulness; follow your own routine once you have established it. Steeping times vary from as little as two or three minutes for strongly flavored ingredients to up to ten for milder. Use your judgment and taste to be your guides. Finally, if you decide to sweeten your tea, it is best to use a natural ingredient, such as honey or unrefined sugar, rather than a synthesized or chemically enhanced ingredient.

- ❖ **Tea vs. Tisane**: these two words are often used interchangeably and for good reason: they refer, essentially, to the same thing. Technically speaking, teas are made with some form of actual tea leaf, from the plant camellia sinensis; this includes white tea, yellow tea, green tea, and black tea (oolong is a tea; jasmine is a green tea that has been perfumed with jasmine flowers). Tisanes, on the other hand, are infusions of dried herbs and other edible parts of plants and spices in hot water (herbal teas are technically tisanes). True teas will contain caffeine, in amounts that vary according to color (the darker the tea, the higher the amount of caffeine in almost all cases). Herbal teas do not contain caffeine. The temperature of the water used, as well as the time of steeping, varies according to ingredients; most teas are steeped at lower temperatures than tisanes. Use your judgement and taste preference as guides. For the purposes of this text, all teas and tisanes will be grouped under the name of "tea."

❖ **Tinctures**: these preparations are somewhat similar to teas in that they require herbs and other edible ingredients to be steeped in liquid. However, a tincture is a much more powerful brew, like a concentrated extract. Tinctures are made by soaking lots of herbs and other ingredients in alcohol for a long period of time. Tinctures are made to be used by the drop, rather than by the cupful (that would be dangerous!). They are available at many retail forums, but you can make your own. This requires an abundance of herbs, some high-proof alcohol, a clear glass container, and time. You probably don't need to make more than a half cup of any particular tincture at one time, as it will lose efficacy over time and a little bit goes a very long way. Wash and dry your herbs, if using fresh, and place them in a jar that can be sealed; add an equal amount of high-proof neutral alcohol that is safe for consumption (80-100 proof vodka or other clear grain spirit is ideal). If using dried, change the ratio to one part herbs to four parts alcohol (dried herbs are more concentrated in flavor and potency). Thus, if making about half a cup of tincture, use half a cup each of fresh herbs and alcohol, or two tablespoons of dried herbs to half a cup of alcohol. Seal this jar tightly and let steep for about six weeks, shaking it occasionally. Once the mixture has steeped, strain the tincture into a clean container for storage. Be sure to label it carefully, with date and names of ingredients, as well as proof of spirits used. Keep away from children, of course, as this could be toxic (and certainly the alcohol is not recommended) in large doses. When using, measure out a few drops with an eye dropper. In some instances, tinctures can be administered directly underneath the tongue; in others, they are added to teas or other brews for additional boost. In the recipes below, any tincture required is listed in how many drops to add.

- ❖ **Health Tea**: for a general health tea that provides a boost to the immune system while tasting quite nice, try this recipe: mix one tablespoon of black tea with two teaspoons *each* of dried fennel, hops, and rose hips and one teaspoon *each* of dried elder flower and mint. Steep for three-four minutes, and sweeten, if you like, with honey. A splash of milk or cream would also be appropriate and is soothing to the digestion and good for the skin.

- ❖ **Stress Tea**: Here are two different recipes for assisting in the alleviation of stress and increasing relaxation; these are good to sip before bedtime, of course. The first recipe requires nothing outside of your garden or pantry, really: mix one teaspoon *each* of dried sage, thyme, marjoram, and chamomile, then steep in one cup of not quite boiling water for five minutes. This will be powerful in its taste and probably requires a bit of sweetener for pleasance. This second recipe is similar but might require a bit of additional shopping: mix one ounce *each* of dried lemon balm (or lemon verbena) and chamomile with half an ounce of St. John's wort; steep two tablespoons of the resulting mixture in a cup of nearly boiling water and steep for ten minutes before straining. Keep the rest of the mixture on hand for future use.

❖ **Love Tea**: drinking this tea in combination with performing a particular love spell or ritual can enhance your results. Combine one tablespoon of dried cranberries with two teaspoons *each* of dried hibiscus flowers and dill and one teaspoon *each* of dried fennel and mint. Steep in a cup of nearly boiling water for about five minutes before straining. Because the dried cranberries are somewhat sweet themselves, you may not need additional sweetener, but if you do, use honey as it strengthens the love spell. Hibiscus flowers can be found in any Hispanic grocery store.

❖ **Protection Tea**: this is a good tea to drink for both physical and psychic fortification; as such, it is perfect to make during the advent of cold and flu season, as well as for assistance if you are wading into hostile waters (traveling for work, say, or visiting relatives whose bad energy is disruptive). Mix a tablespoon of mild black tea, such as English breakfast tea, with two teaspoons *each* of dried burdock root and elder flowers and one teaspoon *each* of comfrey, valerian, and hyssop. Steep in a cup of nearly boiling water for three-four minutes and sweeten as you like.

❖ **Purification Tea**: to cleanse and purify your body and spirit, try this tea, especially useful before performing complicated spells or embarking on Sabbat rituals. Mix one tablespoon black tea with two teaspoons *each* chamomile, valerian, and fennel and one teaspoon of hyssop. Steep for five minutes, then sweeten if you like.

❖ **For Digestion**: many teas aid in digestion, but this one is for when you feel your tummy is in need of special healing. Mix equal parts mint, ginger, marjoram, and chamomile—these can be fresh or dried, but remember that dried will be much more concentrated. Steep a heaping tablespoon of this, along with two drops of elderberry tincture, in a cup of nearly boiling water for about ten minutes.

❖ **For Fever**: this strong tea both warms you from the inside out, and conversely, reduces inflammation and fever. Mix equal parts dried cinnamon, marjoram, and thyme. Use a heaping tablespoon of this mixture per one cup of nearly boiling water and steep for about ten minutes.

- ❖ **For Colds**: this should help with preventing or reducing the effects of the common cold during the winter months. Mix one ounce *each* of dried blackberry, mint, elder flowers, and linden flowers. Use a heaping tablespoon of this mixture per one cup of nearly boiling water and steep for about ten minutes.

- ❖ **For Energy**: when you need a boost to get going, especially in the cooler months, this tea will help you out. Combine one part *each* of dried cinnamon, ginger, and crushed coriander seeds with *either* two parts fresh citrus peel (preferably orange) *or* three drops orange tincture.

- ❖ **Some Basic Herbal Teas**: steeping fresh **mint** and honey in nearly boiling water is a ritual practiced throughout the Middle East; not only is this concoction simple, bracing, and refreshing, it is also an excellent digestive boost and protective brew in and of itself—add some lemon for extra purification power. Throughout Asia, **barley tea** is routinely ingested for health benefits: To enjoy at home, toast ¼ whole (not pearled) barley in a medium hot skillet for about 10 minutes. Meanwhile, bring about 1 quart of water to a boil. When barley is done toasting, add it to the water and lower heat. Bring to a bare simmer for 15 minutes, then strain. This tea is lovely served with a touch of honey to sweeten. This technique is also used with brown rice. **Cinnamon teas** are also excellent for health and energy: Combine 8 sticks of cinnamon with 1 quart of water and ½ cup sugar. Heat to a boil, then lower heat and simmer for about 20 minutes. Fish out the cinnamon sticks and serve. This tea is often served cold, garnished with a spoonful of pine nuts. Last, **fruit teas** made by steeping dried fruits or peels in boiling water are popular throughout the world. Yuzu tea is incredibly popular throughout Asia, for one example, and adding dried berries to any true tea is an excellent way to add health benefits in addition to flavor—blueberries, raspberries, and cranberries are good bets.

Chapter 7
Practical Magic: Preparing Oils

Essential oils are utilized in many aspects of Wiccan practice and ritual; as with other forms of herbal magic, the use of essential oils dates back centuries and were common to shamans and religious practitioners of various stripes. Infusing various herbs and other plant materials into oil was a way in which to harness and amplify their energy signals, allowing them to become concentrated and versatile. Oils are versatile in that, depending on how they are prepared, they can be administered in potions and other edible brews, applied to candles and crystals in the casting of spells, and/or administered to anoint ritual tools and incense. Their intense scent is an inherent part of their magical potency, and their widely applicable nature makes them as essential to your practice as their very name suggests.

Typically, essential oils are made by infusing some part of a plant—leaves, roots, stems, bark, seeds—in a carrier oil also made of natural ingredients (olives, sesame, grapeseed). Certain types were clearly considered sacred (remember the frankincense and myrrh of the Biblical tales?) and were made using basic ingredients and rudimentary methods. With today's technology, the range of essential oils has exploded, as steam distillation and other processing methods can produce powerful essential oils with a wider variety of ingredients. Most of these kinds of essential oils are *not* edible; they are used in aromatherapies and other holistic healing rituals. The kinds of essential oils that you can prepare at home—mostly of the edible variety—will be less overwhelming and potent, but are incredibly useful in the kitchen, for potions and teas and the like.

When seeking out essential oils, be sure to check the provenance: oils made with synthetic ingredients simply will not be as effective (or effective at all) in most Wiccan applications. This is because what imbues the oils with magical power is the life force of the herbs, plants, and other ingredients that go into them; the use of synthetic materials may create something that is pleasing to smell, but it certainly won't have the energy that organic materials will boast. The other consideration here is the oil itself: the oil is the medium through which the living energy and properties of the organic material is amplified and transferred; thus, it should also be as natural as possible.

The most significant power of essential oils resides in its ability to amplify scent, the mysterious sense that heightens our minds and connects us to higher realms with just a whiff. This is why incense, candles, and the liberal use of essential oils are so crucial to many Wiccans; the power of aroma to heighten our senses, open our minds, and generate a particular atmosphere conducive to particular kinds of intentions cannot be underestimated. These oils allow practitioners to promote a kind of deep inner focus that often cannot be achieved without some assistance. When channeling the energies of the universe and nature, it is best to engage all of the senses and honor all of the elements. Essential oils are another important tool to do just that.

To make essential oils that can be used in teas and other digestible potions, see Chapter 10 on The Wiccan Kitchen. To understand and make your own essential oils and blends for candles, incense, and other anointing functions—to use them for the power of their life force and carrier scent—see below for some guidelines on what kinds of oils promote particular properties and how to blend for use in spellwork and other magic.

❖ First, as stated above, be sure to procure any oils that you use from researched and reputable sources so that you know that they are natural and potent. When making your own blends, you will need not only your essential oil but also a neutral carrier oil, such as olive or grapeseed, in order to dissolve the various oils into it. It's also a good idea to invest in a funnel for transferring your blends to storage jars, which can be any clean glass container but apothecary jars with stoppers for dispensing oils are ideal. Most oils lose their potency after a year or so; thus, only purchase as much as you think you will use in that time.

❖ **Prosperity Oil**: this can be used in any spell designed to attract money or abundance; combined in a ritual with jade stone and anointing green good fortune candles will bring out this blend's highest potency. Combine two tablespoons neutral carrier oil with four drops of patchouli essential oil, three drops of bergamot, two drops of cypress, and one drop of lavender.

❖ **Love & Attraction Oil**: this particular oil is designed more for romantic and passionate use, rather than platonic application; it can also promote lasting bonds between two partners. Combine two tablespoons neutral carrier oil with three drops *each* of ginger essential oil and patchouli essential oil, then add one drop *each* of rosemary oil, lavender oil, and sandalwood oil.

❖ **Energy Oil**: use this blend when you want to reinvigorate yourself, physically, psychically, or sexually. Combine two tablespoons neutral carrier oil with three drops of vanilla essential oil and one drop *each* of cinnamon oil and clove oil. The best way to use this oil is to anoint incense or a candle with it, so you inhale the fumes while meditating on your intention.

❖ **Purification Oil**: use this when clearing negative energy out of a space or to anoint a candle or bath when practicing personal cleansing. Combine two tablespoons neutral carrier oil with five drops of juniper essential oil, three drops cedarwood, and one drop lavender.

❖ You can also pair crystals with essential oils made from botanical products to great effect. Here are some ideas of good pairings between the two:

- To promote optimism, spray grapefruit oil onto citrine stone and place it on your altar or other prominent spot in the home.
- To bolster self-esteem, anoint moonstone or jade with bergamot oil; this provides uplift and confidence. An excellent way to employ this pairing is to anoint a piece of moonstone or jade jewelry that you have with the bergamot oil (jasmine is also good) and wear it until the scent wears off. Recharge your crystal and repeat, when necessary.
- To promote physical energy, purify some lace agate with lemon or peppermint oil; this combination of stone and oil boosts energy and desire for activity. If you have an exercise room or designated duffel bag, this would be a good place to have these amplified stones on hand.
- To promote healthful eating, anoint malachite with peppermint oil (or essence of vanilla—not an actual essential oil but also appropriate) and keep it on your dining table. The malachite promotes positive change while peppermint oil is both refreshing and a natural appetite suppressant.
- To promote joyfulness, spray jasper with orange oil and carry it with you in a pocket or purse. They both bring the effusive joyfulness of sunlight to your energy.

- To reconnect with nature, infuse sunstone with essential pine oil. This, of course, is in the case that you cannot actually be outside, such as in the deepest storms of winter or when stuck in an office. This is excellent to have on your desk to keep feelings of nature about you.
- To enhance relationships, romantic or platonic, use ylang-ylang oil to anoint a garnet. This promotes a deepening of the bond in a relationship and is especially good as a gift to the partner or friend with whom you wish to develop a more meaningful bond.
- To promote the spirit of service, spray jasper with rosewood oil, which reminds us that our worth is derived from what we give to others, as well as fostering feelings of empathy for others.
- To cultivate gratitude, use marjoram oil to anoint moss agate. The former brings joyful memories, while the latter keeps us grounded and balanced.
- To promote psychic connection, use frankincense to anoint turquoise, a typical healing combination but one that also promotes openness to the spiritual world.

❖ The powerful combination of crystals and herbs (and their attendant elements, plants and spices) can even help us to get rid of the worst habits, like addiction (to smoking, drinking, eating, and so on). In a large fireproof pot—or cauldron, if you have one—combine cinnamon, ginger and chile powder in equal quantities and place on top of a piece of charcoal. Put a red candle to one side of the pot and a black candle to the other side and anoint with frankincense essential oil; encircle the pot or cauldron with citrine, amethyst, and/or clear quartz. Light the red candle, acknowledging that red is a strong, powerful color; say a chant if you like: *"Red is the color of strength, red is the color of power. I have the strength to kick this habit, day by day, hour by hour."* Then, light the black candle, noting that this color banishes negativity: *"Black is the color that sends things away, and gives me the power to kick this today."* Then, ignite the spice/charcoal pile and, once it is smoldering well, drop onto something that signifies what bad habit or addiction you wish to break (part of a cigarette pack, food or alcohol wrapper, or even a piece of paper with the habit written and crossed out). Let that burn out while the candles burn down, then purify the space with a sage smudging.

Chapter 8

Practical Magic: Preparing Baths

One of the most wonderful things about Wiccan practice is the importance of health and well-being through the emphasis on self-care. There is nothing more invigorating, physically and spiritually, than practicing the magic of an herbal bath. Water itself is one of the four elemental forces for which we should be thankful, and its power is nearly unmatched; think of water's power to carve great canyons into the earth over time. That kind of strength is passed along to you when appreciated in a ritual way, and the herbal magic you can apply adds an additional, earthy layer to the mix. Thus, a ritual bath is not only cleansing, but it can also be grounding—and exhilarating and soothing and healing, not necessarily all at the same time. Whatever your intention, preparing a ritual bath with herbs (often in combination with other ritual tools or ingredients) can be a powerful act of magic and self-care. Some ideas for how to prepare baths, as well as some specific recipes for particular intentions follow below.

❖ First, when using herbs in baths, be sure to engage in some sort of method of containment: that is, it's not particularly healthy or cleanly to scatter loose herbs into the bathwater; you risk ending up with minute bits of herbs where you may not wish them to be, as well as to potentially create a mess in the tub. Instead, use sachets of herbs—cheesecloth is readily available and perfectly acceptable to use for ritual baths; just tie the cloth around whatever bundle of ingredients you are using and let it steep in the bath for a few minutes before climbing in. Cheesecloth has the added advantage of being washable: discard the used herbs and such from within and lay the cheesecloth flat in your dishwasher (putting glasses and other items on top of it; the porousness will allow the soap and rinsing to penetrate). Or, you can wash it by hand.

❖ Another way in which to add herbal healing, cleansing, and other magical properties to your bath is to use herbal essential oils (discussed at length in previous chapter). A few drops in your bathwater can stimulate the senses and mind in various ways. Just be judicious in your usage, and be sure you don't consume any essential oils as they can be toxic.

❖ When participating in a ritual bath of any kind, there are a few fundamental guidelines you should follow: first, be sure to take your regular bath or shower before you embark on your ritualized bath; second, avoid using perfumed or chemically enhanced products before you take your ritual bath (lotions, sprays, make-up and the like); third, when you complete your ritual bath, allow yourself to air dry, rather than using a towel. You don't want to rub away the energy that you have just drawn to yourself in submersing in charged water.

❖ Also, be aware of water temperature: you want the bath to be pleasantly warm but not disconcertingly hot. First of all, water that is too hot can scald the skin and even cause nausea and dizziness. Second, water that is too hot can damage the delicate energy of certain herbs; just as when making teas, you want to infuse energy not cook it.

❖ If you don't have the time or resources to take a bath (some small apartments and homes only come equipped with a shower stall), then you can take a ritual shower. This is less common, of course, and some might suggest that it's less powerful, but this, in the end, is in the eye—and intention—of the beholder. Place a bundle of fresh or dried herbs (a mix designed to bring about whatever intention you are trying to manifest) and hang them from the showerhead. The steam from the water will release the aromatic essences and energies of the herbs for you to breathe in and utilize. You can also make use of your essential oil blends in this manner, by placing a few drops of a particular blend (see previous chapter for some basic ideas) into your shampoo or liquid soap. This is another way to utilize herbs in cleansing and protection rituals.

❖ **Bath "Teas"**: Bath teas are very simple sachets that you can make and float in the bath when you want to bring about particular energies. There are any number of combinations that you can make yourself; the following are some examples of particular sachets you can make for your ritual baths. They should all be mixed up using equal parts of each ingredient to make about a half cup's worth of ingredients to use in one bath.

- o To relieve stress, combine valerian, calamus, and lavender
- o To help circulate energy, combine marigold, nettle, and ginger
- o To promote beauty and attraction, combine lavender, rosemary, thyme, mint, and comfrey
- o To restore physical health after an illness or other abuse to the body, combine sage, mugwort, agrimony, and chamomile
- o To relieve inflammation and agitation, combine alder, dandelion, and mint
- o For an all-purpose bath sachet to help you regain your power and indulge in general self-care, combine one teaspoon *each* of dried lavender, rose petals, lemon balm, rosemary, and mint, then anoint this mixture with two drops *each* of lavender essential oil, patchouli oil, and rose oil. Meditate on your specific intentions while you are soaking in the bath, and this will help you manifest those in time.

❖ **Bath "Soaps"**: These "soaps" are homemade concoctions that combine purchased items with some herbal and essential oil remedies that can help you in all kinds of ritual intention. Customize with your own ideas using the Tables of Correspondence in Chapter 11 for further guidelines of what herbs contain what properties.

o Into three ounces of liquid shea butter soap (you can carefully microwave the solid form if you cannot locate liquid without additives), pour about one third of an ounce almond oil and three drops *each* frankincense essential oil and orange essential oil. This both energizes your spirit and increases your attractiveness to positive energies. To portion it out, you can place in small food molds or ice cube trays, freeze, then use a cube at a time to infuse your bathwater.

o For a calming ritual bath, combine one large bunch of fresh lavender with a small bottle of body wash or shampoo (dual purpose would be ideal), letting this steep in a sunny place for a few days. Then, add about five drops of lavender essential oil to the mixture after you have strained out the fresh lavender (discard that). Use as a bubble bath for relaxation and serenity.

o For a ritual cleanse, you can make your own exfoliating soap using oatmeal and herbs. Grate a bar of the purest soap you can find (Ivory is a good choice) into a small bowl, then add two or three tablespoons of oatmeal, and a tablespoon *each* of dried basil and lemon peel. Mix in enough maple syrup to bring ingredients together, and microwave carefully until melted together. Put into molds until solidified, then use when you need a full cleansing bath.

❖ **Bath "Salts"**: These concoctions are not the infamous and rather seedy bath salts that have recently come to be associated with drug abuse and psychoses. Rather, these are concoctions that mix together minerals and herbs in order to create powerfully cleansing and/or energizing results.

   o To increase psychic connections, make this concoction and use it for a ritual bath during the full moon for best results. Combine one cup salt (coarse sea salt or Epsom salt) with ten drops *each* of sandalwood essential oil and lotus essential oil, along with a pinch of dried orris root powder (the dried, powdered form of an iris bulb). This makes enough for two ritual baths.

   o For a ritual bath that will both cleanse and calm the spirit, combine half cup *each* sea salts and Epsom salts (if you can find dead sea salts, by all means use some of that, as well) with forty drops of lavender essential oil. Use about a quarter cup per bath.

❖ Finally, don't limit yourself to herbal baths alone; combining herbs with other tools and ingredients in the Wiccan cupboard creates incredibly powerful results. The following is a basic bath idea that can help you manifest nearly any intention. Gather three pieces of clear quartz, one piece of citrine, a bay leaf, and a half cup of honey mixed with two cups of milk. Place the crystals in the tub while adding gradually warming water; when your tub is about halfway full, add the milk and honey mixture to allow it to warm and mix with the rest of the bathwater. While the bath is filling, write your intention or an appropriate symbol onto the bay leaf, then float it on the surface of the water. Spend at least twenty minutes in the bathwater, envisioning your intention and how you will feel after it is manifested. Certainly, you can use candles and incense, as well, if you'd like.

Remember that self-care, while often equated with indulgence and excess, is actually one of the most important things you can do for yourself. If you allow yourself to become too tired, too physically or emotionally sick to care for yourself, then your energy is too depleted to take care of anyone or anything else. The ritual bath is not an indulgence; rather, it is an act of empowering self-care, a way to recharge your spiritual batteries and to re-energize your overall health and well-being. This kind of self-care should become a regular part of your powerful Wiccan practice.

Chapter 9

Practical Magic: Preparing Incense & Other Herbal Combinations

Herbal magic extends to every branch and ritual within Wiccan practice, and as such, it is widely utilized in combination with other tools and spells in the Wiccan toolkit. Incense is one such significant way in which herbal magic is employed; the highly aromatic scents of herbal incense increase focus and spiritual power, allowing the Wiccan to achieve their highest intentions. Incense is indispensable to most Wiccan practice. Herbs are also excellent when combined with crystals and stones—other powerful carriers of spiritual and natural energy—and can be used in any number of spells of just about any variety.

Herbal Incense

❖ Incense has, since ancient times, been considered a conduit between the spiritual and the physical realm; it allows the practitioner to communicate with forces beyond the physical. Representing the element of air, primarily, incense allows us not only to focus our intentions but also to send our message out into the far firmament. Its power to spread messages makes it routine in ritual use.

❖ While our contemporary use of incense has been dominated by commercially produced sticks or cones for ease and convenience, the most traditional ways in which incense was used was to burn herbs, leaves, bark, and other organic matter in a censer that was hung above the ritual space or swung back and forth to disseminate the aromatic smoke to all gathered (you can still see this kind of usage in traditional religious ceremonies, such as in some Greek Orthodox and Catholic churches). Some Wiccans also clear a space on their altar for a censer—or, sometimes, an actual cauldron—wherein they place their herbs and other ingredients to burn for ritual practice or spellwork. Using these more traditional methods allows for the practitioner to customize the blend of herbs in order to manifest specific messages and intentions.

❖ Additionally, incense can be used as an offering to deities, spirits, or elements (always practice caution with flame and burning, so don't ever leave the offering and walk away). Some Wiccans meditate to their burning incense, practicing the art of divination and/or psychic connection.

❖ If you decide to purchase incense—which you probably will stock your altar with at least some purchased incense—be sure to check the provenance of the source, as you want an incense that is close to natural as possible. Also be sure not to buy incense that will trigger allergies or other potential reactions; it's always best to source it in person so that you know exactly how it will smell. You can also purchase a relatively neutral incense and enhance its aroma and effectiveness by anointing it with essential oils or blends.

❖ When using "raw" incense—that which you procure and sprinkle directly onto coals—understand these advantages: using raw incense means that you control the amount of smoke that is created, as well as where it is directed, so consider the four cardinal directions in addition to the overall intention of the ritual or spell; when you create your own incense, you also control what kinds of intentions you emit at different times during the ritual (sage for purification at the beginning; basil for a protective spell; jasmine for serenity at end—for an example); last, incense cones and sticks last for a more limited amount of time, while the coals used to burn raw incense can last for an hour or more.

❖ Once you decide to make your own incense, stock up on a variety of ingredients:

   o Obviously, you should have herbs, and these should be dried not fresh. Fresh herbs don't burn readily and can create billows of acrid smoke if they do burn, so dried is what you want here. Don't forget that the category of herbs also includes flowers and such.

o Resins are another powerful ingredient that can help your homemade incense come together. Made from the dried sap of trees and plants, these resins provide a long, slow burn, in addition to adding their own particular properties. Some common resins include frankincense and mastic.

o Woods can also be used to make incense—but not just any bark from any tree in your neighborhood. First, sourcing locally might mean that you are burning chemicals that may have been sprayed on the trees or in the area. Second, fresh wood, like fresh herbs, does not burn well. Instead, seek out fragrant dried wood, such as cedar and sandalwood; these also have magical properties of their own.

o Roots, again in dried form, can be employed to good use in incense, particularly in incense intended for rituals and spellwork associated with the earth element or the Mother Goddess.

o Spices are also frequently used in incense, from cinnamon and vanilla to allspice and fennel. Seeds, berries, and barks of all kinds can impart particular properties as well as tantalizing aromas for all kinds of practice. Dried citrus peel is another common ingredient, roughly categorized in this case as a spice.

- Essential oils are also sometimes added to incense, either to increase the potency of the aroma or to add an additional property important to the intention.

- Finally, you will also want to invest in a mortar and pestle and/or a spice grinder (the former being preferable, because made of stone, typically) to grind all of your incense ingredients together into a rough powder ready to burn atop coals. Incense coals are usually available at shops that sell Wiccan merchandise.

❖ Try the following recipe for homemade incense that you can use for many basic rituals; it will provide protective elements, as well as increase spiritual communication and banish negative energies. You can use measurements as small as teaspoons or as large as cups, as long as the ratios are roughly the same (and your mortar and pestle can reasonably hold the ingredients). Put four parts frankincense into your mortar first and pound the gummy substance for a bit; it's the hardest part to break down so you should get it nicely smooth before adding your other ingredients. Now add one part *each* vervain, mugwort, and rose; add half parts cedar and cinnamon; add one quarter part bay laurel. Grind this all together into a rough powder. Label recycled jars and store indefinitely. When using, be sure to ignite your incense coal—don't use regular coal, or you risk carbon monoxide poisoning—in a flameproof censer, cauldron or other container. These coals will get extremely hot, so be sure that you handle everything with great care once they are burning. Add about a half teaspoon of your incense to the coals, sprinkling with additional if necessary. Be sure to snuff out coals completely when done, or douse with water if coal is sufficiently burned up (if you plan to re-use coal, don't wet it).

Using Herbs with Other Tools

❖ As discussed in Chapter 4, crystals and stones can be incredibly useful in creating a flourishing garden. Moss and tree agate stones are two of the most useful stones in cultivating gardens. They work on both the gardener and the garden itself: in the first case, these agate stones are said to increase the attunement between the human and plant consciousness, thus allowing for a greater, more positive flow of energy between the two. When you meditate with either of these stones in an outdoor setting, it can bring you closer to the earth element, in general. In the second case, these stones will increase the productivity of the garden, sheltering seeds and promoting growth. This can be achieved by planting the stones at the base of plants or around the perimeter of the garden; you can also build a small altar of the stones at the center of the garden, allowing the energy to radiate outward. In addition, infusing the water can with which you water your garden can also boost yields and encourage positive energy.

❖ Plants in general also have communicative powers that are beyond our simple understanding. It is well known that plants communicate through a variety of methods, through roots and fungi, flowers and seeds. Their symbiosis with other species (of plant, of animal, of mineral) is unparalleled, and through eons of evolution, plants have learned to propagate their species and defend their territories without limbs or central nervous systems. We have much to learn from them with regard to how the larger universe works in interconnected harmony. Herbs are a handy way to lay claim to some of that energy, endow it with intention through crystals, and practice our own healing.

❖ Another specific way in which to combine the energies of crystals and herbs is to make your herbal tinctures and teas with crystal essences—water infused with the energy of particular crystals (see Chapter 7 on how to safely make essences and elixirs with crystals). This enhances the viability of your brew for healing or for love or for whatever other intention you are working to manifest. Use a rose quartz infused essence when brewing a love potion, for example, or a lapis lazuli charged essence into a lavender tea to help with headaches and migraines. Clear quartz, as always, amplifies any energy and intention you might have in mind. You are essentially combining earth elements with water to boost the potency of your herbal medicines.

❖ Crystals are frequently used to turn up psychic and spiritual frequencies, as well, and this can be done in conjunction with connecting to plants, as well, and nature in general. If your garden begins to show signs of disease or distress, this is an excellent way to channel healing energy to it: leave stones as offerings to the spirits at the four cardinal directions within the garden; meditate on your intentions and recognize the flow of energy between yourself and the plants.

❖ Use crystals in herbal smudging rituals, as well. Build a small stone altar with a clear quartz anchor and a surrounding cast of tourmaline or obsidian; carefully ignite your dried herb bundle (sage is often at least one part of this) over the stones (be sure to have a fireproof anchor of some sort underneath it for safety), then envision that you are receiving the energy from the stones up through your herb bundle and waft it through the room. This process both clears the area of negative energy, as well as infuses it with the grounded earthen energy from the crystal altar. Basically, you are purging the bad and channeling the good.

❖ Make a cleansing face steam using dried herbs and flowers, such as lavender and rose petals. Put two clear quartz crystals (or one clear and one rose, for love) into a large bowl and scatter your dried herbs and flowers about—a variety is good, but the two suggestions above will also work fine on their own. Pour over a quantity of very hot water—be sure to use crystals that are strong enough to withstand high temperatures—then lean your face over, covering your head with a towel so that the steam doesn't escape. This is purifying and refreshing, a weekly beauty routine with positive energy to spare.

❖ Put your crystals and dried herbs at work in protecting and promoting good energy as you work: sew small crystals and herb bundles into the seams of your apron for kitchen work or into the pockets of pants or overalls that you use for outdoor work in the garden or otherwise. Choose stones for luck and abundance, with herbs like basil for protection.

❖ Herbs can also be included in your crystal cleansing baths—or in your daily shower: hang a bunch of fresh herbs—rosemary, lavender, and mint—combined with some fresh eucalyptus fronds from your shower head. These will work to cleanse alongside whatever intention you have for your crystals during your ritual bath. These can stay in the shower for several days to weeks, depending on how fresh they are and how damp they get. Be sure to recycle them into your compost pile when they have lost their freshness. Return that energy to the ground!

❖ Connect with your ancestors using the combination of obsidian and bay leaf (this is only one possible combination, but a good one): write a symbol onto the bay leaf, something that represents a particular ancestor or simply calls to mind ancestral spirits, and place it outdoors under a full moon. Leave it be until the moon has waned to its smallest crescent, meditating each night on the ancestral forces you wish to connect with.

Herbs are excellent fodder for all sorts of magical objects, such as sachets and dream pillows or homemade incense and oils. Combining these with crystals makes their potential magic more powerful: drop in a small clear quartz crystal in your herbal sachet to amplify its potency; keep an amethyst under your herbal dream pillow for more psychic energy; use a cut crystal as an incense holder. You need only study and understand the different powers and energies possessed by various herbs to begin to utilize them in everyday Wiccan practice and in occasional ritual or celebration.

Chapter 10

The Wiccan Kitchen: Recipes for Empowerment, Love, Success, and Luck

There is nothing quite so magical as the kitchen: it is the central gathering place in any dwelling, as anyone who has hosted a dinner party knows. No matter how hard you try to herd guests out of the kitchen, it turns out to be the place where everyone wants to be. That should come as no surprise, really, because the kitchen abounds with lovely aromas, beautiful sights, and hums with the energy of transformation—because that, at its heart, is what cooking is all about, transforming a handful of elements into something tasty, nourishing, and literally soul-sustaining. Thus, it is only natural that Wiccan practitioners gravitate toward the kitchen, as well, for Sabbat feasts, daily sustenance, and the conjuring of intention. Read on for an understanding of the kitchen's role in history and belief, as well as the power of food and drink to transform our consciousness, followed by some recipes to bring you self-power, love, success, and luck.

Home and Hearth: The Magical Kitchen

There is no denying that fire and the hearth—and the food they produce—are absolutely central to the development of the community of humankind. The rise of family groups which turned to clans which eventually became nation-states: this began around the hearth, with the ritual breaking of bread. Fire itself functions as a beacon, lighting the way and calling people to it; ritual ceremonies would not be complete without fire and food. Our spiritual experiences also originate, in large part, from fire and hearth: ritual offerings of meat were once a part of many cultures' typical experience, and the rules concerning what we eat and how we eat have always been a deeply religious concern. Thus, any undertaking of spiritual practice—whether it be mainstream religion, personal preference, or Wiccan ritual—is suffused with the traditions of fire and food. The aforementioned "breaking of bread" is no mere metaphor; it is the literal representation of how we create and maintain a community, of how we manifest caring and love. It is no coincidence that Wiccans celebrate the Mother Goddess with such reverence, for she is the giver of sustenance, both from the land and from her body itself.

Consider the rituals surrounding food in which we still partake, consciously or not, with spiritual intent or secular ceremony. Feasting is not a relic of some bygone past, nor is the idea that food brings with it certain medicinal benefits and healing powers. Communion is taken in many Christian churches, one of the ultimate expressions of sacrifice within a spiritual community. Religious holidays and secular festivals are celebrated with feasting and abundance: Easter hams or Passover legs of lamb; Thanksgiving turkeys and Fourth of July barbecues; Samhain celebrations and Halloween trick-or-treating. These are all examples of the ways in which food plays a central role in our secular and spiritual experience. Even sitting down together at a daily family meal holds a special magic, if all the sociological evidence is to be trusted: kids who eat dinner with family (and sans electronic devices) on a regular basis do better academically, socially, and developmentally. There is no substitute for the magic of the kitchen.

With regard to Wiccan practice, the kitchen also holds a special place, connecting belief to the past and keeping it rooted in the present. For those Wiccans who embrace the witch and witchcraft associations, the kitchen is especially ripe with symbology, as witches brew their potions with magical herbs and hefty cauldrons. Indeed, many modern-day Wiccans and witches own their own cauldron, imbuing it with magical energy to make powerful potions for love, for prosperity, for luck, and for healing, among any number of other intentions.

In addition, it is important not to lose sight of the crucial role the natural world plays in the understanding and undertaking of Wiccan practice: the cycle of the seasons and the phases of the moon determine the entire calendar of Wiccan practice and ritual; these cyclical energies are what give rise to the rebirth of spring and the renewing of the land, the high season of summer productivity, and the bountiful fall harvest. Even in winter, the ground lies dormant but does not die; it is but a moment's sunlight and warmth in February to coax the first herbs of the season out of their slumber. Thus, it is no surprise that much of Wiccan practice and ritual employs the use of herbs, plants, foods, and feasts. These things all reconnect us to the earth from which we get our strongest and most lasting energy. Combine that with the power of the hearth—fire, water, earthly minerals, and life's breath—for transformation, and the kitchen becomes the encapsulation of what Wiccan core beliefs suggest. Interconnectedness, positive energies, natural elements, and magical transformation; the kitchen can quickly become our spiritual center.

Once you begin your Wiccan practice, you may decide that the kitchen is a place of special energy for you. If that is the case, then there are numerous ways that you can apply your new-found beliefs and energies in that space. See the following list for some examples of how the kitchen can express your Wiccan energy.

- ❖ Cooking with particular intention need not rely on a special recipe or the use of specific ingredients; magical cooking can transpire whenever you imbue the moment with intention and mystery.
- ❖ Even completing kitchen chores, as mundane as they may seem, can fortify your Wiccan practice, if you do them with

purpose and energy. It can be seen as both a process of purification and an exercise in protection.

❖ Creating sachets of aromatic herb and other ingredients can enhance your intention and imbue the space with positive aroma and energy. You can even tuck herbs into various corners of your kitchen, or sew them into cloth napkins and tablecloths.

❖ Organize your kitchen with some basic Wiccan principles in mind: facing north is where the earth energy lies, while fire faces south, water faces west, and air faces east. The ideas within the eastern practice of Feng Shui would also work in said organization.

❖ In the spirit of organization, keep cabinets and drawers organized with tools and materials within easy view and reach. Spices and herbs often get thrown into a cabinet wherein you must hunt around for what you want: instead, set aside a deep kitchen drawer for your collection of jars, putting labels on the top; this way, you can pull out the drawer and easily see everything at a glance. This kind of organization encourages the free flow of energy and spirit.

❖ Hang wind chimes that you have blessed in your kitchen (if feasible, to the east to honor the wind) for protection and the flow of good energy.

❖ Think about purchasing (or making) kitchen utensils out of natural materials, rather than plastics or other manmade elements.

* There is no rule that you must have only one altar: create a kitchen altar with a prominent image of the Mother Goddess as provider. This will oversee all of your kitchen rituals and tasks.

* Bring your ritual into the kitchen, when appropriate. Candles and scented oils certainly have a place (as long as they don't overpower the aromas of food preparation), as do meaningful symbols, talismans, and amulets.

* Cook with the seasons. So many contemporary cooks, lured by the artificial provenance of commercial grocery stores and big box marts, have forgotten what it's like to pay attention to the passing of the seasons in the kitchen. Cook with fresh, seasonal, and ideally local ingredients, and you are truly practicing Wiccan magic in the kitchen.

* Better yet, start your own kitchen garden. With nothing more than a few inexpensive tools and easily sourced materials, you can easily grow your own herbs and even some vegetables in a small raised bed or in some containers. This connects you both to the land and to the seasons in an even deeper, more conscious manner. Plus, homegrown food is inexpensive, satisfying, and infinitely tastier than anything you can buy in a commercial store. Short of that, become a farmers' market regular, where everything is almost as good as homegrown (sometimes better, admittedly), the variety is greater, and the seasonality is assured.

- ❖ Learn the craft of preservation. If you are to connect with nature and the seasons, then you will learn quickly that you always have an abundance of something at any given time of the year. Learning to can, freeze, dehydrate, and ferment are all incredibly powerful crafts. There are some tips and techniques for these methods below.

- ❖ Educate yourself about the typical foods that you keep in your kitchen, particularly herbs and spices, which often have very special uses in Wiccan practice. The more you know about what a particular element can add to your cooking, the better able you are to create meals and feasts and potions with clear intention and best results.

- ❖ Consider the actual actions of cooking: chopping, for example, is a way to release negative energy and cultivate calm. Stirring itself can also have a calming effect.

- ❖ There is also something to be said about the kind of energy that is created by preparing different kinds of food: making a large, hearty stew or roast generates a very different kind of energy than prepping a crisp salad full of leafy greens and fresh vegetables. Make food that assists you in harnessing the kind of energy your intention needs.

- ❖ Remember, too, that food itself can be symbolic: eggs, for example, are indicative of fertility and, as such, are featured during springtime celebrations in a variety of beliefs.

❖ Also remember that kitchen materials can also be used for magic outside of the realm of consumption. Herbal shampoos and soaps, incense and potpourri, aromatic oils and essences can all come out of the kitchen for various uses in other locations.

Tips and Techniques for Using Herbs

Your Wiccan kitchen can provide any number of intentions and inspirations for your practice, ritual, and general belief. The following ideas contain methods of how to prepare and preserve food, with some general recipes for potions and feast foods.

❖ **Preservation**: should you decide to garden or to shop at the farmers' market, you will inevitably need to learn how to preserve when you have an abundance of product. This is also in keeping with the idea of avoiding waste, respecting and giving gratitude to that which nature and the Mother Goddess has granted.

  ○ Some herbs are excellent candidates for **drying**, such as oregano, sage, rosemary, thyme, and mint. Other tender herbs, like parsley and basil, do not particularly well when dried, as they lose their potency of aroma and taste. The absolute easiest way to dry herbs is to clean your bundles carefully, dry them thoroughly, and arrange them on a sheet pan or large tray and put them somewhere out of the way. If your house is climate-controlled, they should dry on their own within a week (if it's too damp where you live, keep an eye out for spoilage). If you experience hot, dry summers, you can also hang your herbs from an outdoor rafter and they'll be dry in no time. Some recommend microwaves for drying, but this can be risky. Natural air drying is best.

o For those herbs that don't take to drying, **infuse** them into oils and vinegars which you can use both for cooking and for ritual practice. With oil, it is best to gently heat a quality oil (extra-virgin olive oil, neutral grapeseed oil, non-GMO peanut oil), then throw in a handful of your herbs, let steep for a few hours, then strain and store. This should keep almost indefinitely. With vinegar, simply steep the herbs in the vinegar, no need to heat or strain.

o Chile peppers and some spices also take well to the above preparations. The Southwest is rife with *ristras*, hanging wreaths of dried or drying red peppers, and these edible ornamentations are also excellent vehicles for channeling good energy and **protection**. Chile oils are also used throughout the world, both for their flavor and for their healing properties.

- You can also pickle or ferment foods to both prolong their shelf-life and to boost their health benefits. Pickled garlic and chiles are commonplace in many parts of the world and offer powerful protection. A very basic pickling brine can be made with equal parts vinegar and water with enough salt to both flavor and promote preservation.
- So, for example, 2 cups of cider vinegar, 2 cups of water, and 1 tablespoon plus a pinch more of kosher salt makes a great basic pickling liquid for about 2 pints worth of vegetables. Bring brine to a boil, stirring to dissolve salt, then pour over vegetables packed in sterilized jars. For variety and flavor, add aromatics, such as garlic cloves and dried peppers; add as much sugar as salt for sweet and sour versions; vary the kind of vinegar used. Many vegetables take well to this, including okra and green beans: don't use sugar and do add garlic and peppers. Make sure, if you aren't canning, to blanch these beforehand. For pickled garlic and cucumbers, use the lighter rice wine vinegar and add some sugar. For a lovely blush color and some natural sweetness, add a peeled and sliced beet to some radishes pickled in this manner.

o For a magical and powerful protective tonic, conjure up the following method: In a sterilized jar, put 4 chopped hot peppers (serrano, jalapeno, Thai, cayenne, or a mix). Add a couple tablespoons of cider vinegar, a teaspoon each of soy sauce and fish sauce, a bay leaf, and a couple of crushed garlic cloves to your peppers. Bring about 10 ounces of water to a boil then poor over the ingredients in jar. Let it cool a bit before refrigerating where it will keep indefinitely. Sprinkle it on plain rice; use it to bring some tart heat to soups, stews, curried and the like; add a shot of it to plain tomato juice or a Bloody Mary. Or just have a sip or two of it after dinner. This tonic brings together symbolic representations of all the elements to create an unbeatable **elixir for power**.

❖ **Potions**: brew or mix some up in the kitchen to bring about particular intentions and results. These potions can be uniquely powerful in that they not only contain ingredients that possess the energy of the intention you wish to create, but they are also concocted following some suggestions of Wiccan practice. Here are three examples of simple potions to brew up in your Wiccan kitchen.

o **For love**, you can try the following method, but do realize that a love potion cannot force a love that is not already present; it merely harnesses the latent energy and helps it to become more present and powerful. Dry flowers and herbs—roses and lavender, for example—by the light of a full moon (be sure to avoid flower shop roses, which are laden with indigestible chemicals), then add fresh spring water to cover stirring clockwise. Flavor the mixture with cinnamon, lemon, and honey—to ignite passion and sweetness—and recite your intention or a specific love spell while you stir seven times. Be clear in your intention. Store in a clear container away from sunlight until the next full moon. This can draw love to you or be given to the one from whom you wish love.

o **For success**, combine dried pine, ginger, cedar, cinnamon, and allspice in a mortar and pestle; grind to a fine powder. Sprinkle yourself (or some kind of symbols of success, such as money or representations of what success means to you) with the powder, reciting your intention and invoking the appropriate dieties. Another recipe for prosperity is to combine a teaspoon each of cinnamon and allspice with half a cup of sugar. Energize the mixture with a charm: "Sugar and spice and all that's nice/ A pinch of magic and a bit of charm/ May my intent turn out well." Use in tea or coffee or anything else that seems appropriate.

o **For luck**, make a pouch with basil, allspice, and star anise to place upon your altar. Give it an all-purpose charm with your intention (luck) being in the chosen materials. Try this: "Enchanted herbs of brown and green/ Herbs for magic and power I deem. / Goddess bless all that I do. / I do no harm to you. / With herb and spice, this charm is thru." The same can be done with different ingredients for different intentions: rosemary and garlic for purification, or marjoram and rosemary for love.

When working in the kitchen, don't limit yourself to thinking in strictly magical or ritual terms: the kitchen itself, by its very nature, is an enchanted place whose function is not merely to brew potions or even cook dinners. Rather, its function is to bring people together in love and peaceful intention. When cooking for yourself or others, consider the make-up of the menu in Wiccan terms: why not add a bit of extra spice to the stew, or throw in a pinch of cinnamon to the marinade? If you've planted your garden, or have your herbs in windowsills, then you have handy— and healing—garnishes at the ready. Also take a page out of the Asian way of thinking about food, which also applies to the Wiccan concept of balance: menus should contain a balance of masculine and feminine energies (yin and yang, in Chinese philosophy), as well as promoting various kinds of energies. Review the chakras in Chapter 2 and consider which foods would be best in promoting positive energy in particular parts of the body. Color, too, can be a consideration, not just for aesthetic purposes but for magical intentions: browns and greens bring earthy tones and good fortune to your cooking, while bright reds (berries and beets) and yellows (turmeric and squash) bring energy to your plate. Every day cooking in a Wiccan kitchen can very easily incorporate the philosophies of Wiccan thinking: preparing and preserving the natural abundance with care and consideration, giving thanks to the spirits, the elements, and the deities is a constant way in which we keep in tune with the natural world, even within our climate-controlled home.

The kitchen is the fundamental place where the magic of daily life can happen on a routine basis. If you arrange it thoughtfully and stock it thoroughly, the kitchen will quickly become the center of your Wiccan home, with abundance, love, and delight doled out in equal proportions—for solitary meals, regular family dinners, and elaborate celebrations alike. Make your home and hearth a comforting and magical place.

Chapter 11

Tables of Correspondence and Workbook

The following tables contain a selected list of herbs, in the first case, and essential oils, in the second place, and their attendant properties: now you can begin to embark on using your own intentions to utilize your garden herbs in ways that meet your own purpose. These lists are just partial, but a strong foundation in commonly used herbs and essential oils, along with explanations of some of their numerous properties and uses. The final document here is a sample of a workbook that you can use to begin building your own repertoire of recipes, spells, and rituals using herbal magic. The example provided gives you a start. Make copies of the workbook page and fill in as you create your own ideas.

Table: Herbal Correspondences

HERB	PROPERTIES	USES
Aloe	Healing, beauty, peacefulness, protection	Healing burns, cuts, scrapes; skin beautifier; protective spells

Basil	Protection and courage, fertility and good fortune	Tea for digestion; protective spells; purification baths
Chamomile	Relaxation and meditation, centering, healing	Tea for sleeping and psychic connection; brings fortune to gardens
Dandelion	Spiritual messages, divination, welcoming	Tonic for imbalance; heals skin afflictions
Eucalyptus	Healing and protection	Add to charms and amulets, as an essential oil
Fennel	Protection, purification, good fortune	Use in money spells; add to purification rituals
Ginger	Power and success, love, wealth	Use in healing teas and love spells
Holly	Protection, love	Use as protection when planted around house; berries for passion
Ivy	Protection	Climbing vines protect homes; good

		luck for a housewarming gift
Jasmine	Peacefulness, love	Use in all manner of love and attraction spells
Lemon	Purification and blessings	Use in cleansing spells and casting a circle
Mint	Money, empowerment, luck, strength	Use in all manner of spells and potions. All-purpose.
Nutmeg	Visions and psychic communication	Use in divination and dream sachets
Orange Peel	Joyfulness, vibrancy, love	Use in love spells and energy teas
Pine	Protection, cleansing, centering	Good in incense and fertility charms
Rosemary	Love, memory, purification	Use in healing teas and love spells; also good for smudging, along with sage
Sandalwood	Purification and protection, healing	Use in an all-purpose incense for its grounding aroma and purification

Thyme	Purification, energy, promotes sleep	Use in healing spells and ritual baths; all-purpose
Vervain	Cleansing and protection	Also good in love charms and prosperity draughts
Wormwood	Protection against negative energy, bad spirits	Good for communication with spiritual realm
Yarrow	Courage, love, divination	Use in marriage rituals and to amplify potency of companion ingredients

Table: Essential Oil Correspondences

ESSENTIAL OIL	PROPERTIES	WORKS WITH
Star Anise	Protection, banishment of negative energies	Lavender, rose, and orange
Bergamot	Money, abundance, wisdom	Frankincense, lemon, lavender, and orange

Cinnamon	Love, protection, psychic connection	Caraway, chamomile, ginger, all citrus, all spice
Dragon's Blood	Love, protection, banishing negative energies	Patchouli, lavender, and rosemary
Eucalyptus	Purification, especially for spaces	Cedarwood, lemon, thyme, rosemary, and lavender
Frankincense	Psychic and spiritual connection, higher consciousness, stress relief	Sandalwood, pine, camphor, and all citrus
Grapefruit	Protection, healing, strength	All citrus, all spices
Lemongrass	Awareness, personal cleansing	Basil, jasmine, fennel, orange, sage, and ylang ylang
Myrrh	Psychic connection, calming, meditation	Frankincense, juniper, thyme, patchouli, and mint
Neroli	Joy and sex, purification	Vanilla and all spice oils
Orange	Banishing depression and attracting joy	Cinnamon, clove, lavender, and myrrh

Patchouli	Physical energy, sex, wealth	Basil, lavender, cassia, bergamot, and myrrh
Rose	Happiness, love, protection, refreshing psyche	Lavender, patchouli, all citrus, and vanilla
Sage	Memory and improving concentration, purification, wisdom	Lemongrass, rosemary, bergamot, and mint
Tea tree	Anti-bacterial, aids in treating depression	Dragon's blood, patchouli, and lavender
Vanilla	Revitalization and energy, sexual attraction	Rose, lavender, and all spice oils
Ylang ylang	Calming and peaceful, sex and love	Rose, jasmine, and bergamot

Sample Workbook

SPELL TITLE	HERBS NEEDED	HOW TO MAKE
Herbal Dream Sachet	Lavender, chamomile, hops, mugwort, and rose	Mix equal parts of all herbs and wrap into a breathable fabric, such as cheesecloth. Place it under your pillow at night to promote peaceful dreams.

Conclusion

The craft and belief system of Wicca is a potent way to reconnect with nature and with energy to unleash positive forces into the world. Its open and fluid attitudes are attractive to a great diversity of people, and its spirituality is designed to promote power and self-care, particularly for women. With an understanding that the goddesses are equal to the gods, as well as recognition of the role of natural forces, Wicca promotes a practice that is egalitarian, rich in process, and filled with satisfying ritual and community.

You have now begun to understand the importance of herbal and plant magic to manifesting your goals and channeling universal energy. One of the most significant parts of Wiccan practice is the use of herbs: these ancient, organic plants have been used across cultures and throughout the centuries for every kind of intention imaginable. Herbs can assist Wiccans in everything from nurturing love to fostering good energy and healing to establishing protection. Herbal magic that is undertaken with respect to the Wiccan rede—do others no harm—provide comfort, success, and self-love for many.

Wicca is, at its very core, an inclusive belief system that emphasizes our relationships with the natural and spiritual realms—herbs being the most natural conductor between those realms. The Mother Goddess and the Horned God bring their energy and wisdom to our lives every day in Wiccan practice. Anyone who wishes to channel their energy into a positive and powerful life of intention and achievement can begin by building an herbal garden, cultivating magical plants, and using them in the kitchen and beyond for every ritual and magical practice.

Made in the USA
Monee, IL
08 October 2020

44299257R00085